❧ Perfect Darling

Stella

Jennie

George

Eileen Quelch

❧ *Perfect Darling*

The Life and Times of
George Cornwallis-West

Cecil & Amelia Woolf • London

Published by C. and A. Woolf
Kingly Court, 10 Kingly Street, London W1

ISBN 0 900821 19 1

❧ Contents

❧ *Illustrations*

❧ *Acknowledgements*

I am indebted to Her Majesty the Queen for her gracious permission to reproduce a letter of Albert Edward Prince of Wales.

I am also grateful to the following for permission to quote from letters in which they hold the copyright: Mr Simon Asquith (J.M. Barrie); Viscount Chandos (the Hon. Mrs Alfred Lyttelton); Mr Peregrine Churchill (Lady Randolph Churchill); Lady Mary Grosvenor (Col William Cornwallis-West); Mr Seymour Leslie (Lady Leslie); the Prince Pless (Daisy Princess of Pless); His Grace the Duke of Portland (the 6th Duke); His Grace the Duke of Westminster (the 2nd Duke); C. & T. Publications (Sir Winston Churchill); the Society of Authors on behalf of the George Bernard Shaw Estate (Shaw letters).

Acknowledgements are also due to the authors, or their trustees, and the publishers, of the following books: Lady Cynthia Asquith, *Diaries* (Hutchinson); Consuelo Vanderbilt Balsan, *The Glitter and the Gold* (William Heinemann); Cecil Beaton, *The Wandering Years* (Weidenfeld & Nicolson); Wilfrid Scawen Blunt, My Diaries (Martin Secker); Mrs Patrick Campbell, *My Life and Some Letters* (Hutchinson); Randolph S. Churchill, *Winston S. Churchill,* volumes 1 and 2 and Companion volumes 1 and 2 (William Heinemann); Winston S. Churchill, *Lord Randolph Churchill, My Early Life and The World Crisis, 1911-1914* (Odhams Press); Marchioness Curzon of Kedleston, *Reminiscences* (Hutchinson); Viscount D'Abernon, *An Ambassa-*

dor of Peace and *Portraits and Appreciations* (Holder & Stoughton); *Diaries* of Daisy Princess of Pless (John Murray); Baroness Agnes de Stoeckl. *Not all Vanity* (John Murray); Elizabeth Eliot, *They all Married Well* (Cassell); G.A. Escoffier, *A Guide to Modern Cookery* (William Heineman) Lille Langtry, *The Days I Knew* (Hutchinson); Anita Leslie *The Fabulous Leonard Jerome* and *Jennie: The Life of Lady Randolph Churchill* (Hutchinson); Seymour Leslie, *The Jerome Connexion* (John Murray); Shane Leslie, *The Film of Memory* (Michael Joseph) and *The End of a Chapter* (Constable); Edward Marsh, *A Number of People* (William Heineman); Dame Nellie Melba, *Melodies and Memories* (Eyre & Spottiswoode); Viscount Mersey, *A Picture of Life* (John Murray); Milford-on-Sea Record Society; *Leaves from the Note-Books of Lady Dorothy Nevill* (Macmillan); Harold Nicolson, *Small Talk* (Constable); Walburga Lady Paget, *Embassies of Other Days* and *In My Tower* (Hutchinson); the 6th Duke of Portland, *Men, Women and Things* (Faber & Faber); Marie Louise Ritz, *César Ritz* (Harrap); Queen Marie of Roumania, *The Story of My Life* (Cassell); *Bernard Shaw and Mrs Patrick Campbell; their Correspondence* (Victor Gollancz); Clare Sheridan, *To the Four Winds* (Andre Deutsch), Osbert Sitwell, *Great Morning* and *Laughter in the Next Room* (Macmillan); Helen Spinola, *Nothing But the Truth* (Victor Gollancz); Angela Thirkwell, *Three Houses* (Oxford University Press); Lady Troubridge, *Memories and Reflections* (William Heineman); Frances Countess of Warwick, *Life's Ebb and Flow* (Hutchinson); and Loelia Duchess of Westminster, *Grace and Favour* (Weidenfeld & Nicolson).

❧ Introduction

George Cornwallis-West, described by the late Randolph Churchill as the handsomest man of his generation, was born of a family who could claim a long descent when they fought with the Black Prince at Crécy and at Poitiers. His mother was a famous Victorian beauty and wit. His sisters, stars in the Edwardian galaxy, married respectively one of Germany's wealthiest princes and England's richest duke.

From childhood he was accustomed to the Prince of Wales dropping in to see his parents and taking an interest in his career. He stalked deer reserved for the Kaiser, hunted bison in Silesian forests, shot over the finest moors, fished some of the most famous rivers and, as a young Guards officer, won the most coveted riding events.

When he was twenty-five he married Jennie, the glamorous American widow of Lord Randolph Churchill and mother of the ambitious young politician, Winston Churchill, who was the same age as himself. When he was thirty-nine he married the celebrated actress, Mrs Patrick Campbell, and played Doolittle to her Eliza while on tour with *Pygmalion* in America.

Pygmalion was a landmark not only in stage history but in the private lives of its author, Bernard Shaw, and of his leading lady, Beatrice Stella Campbell. The years 1912-1914, which culminated for them in its production at His Majesty's Theatre, coincided with the height of Shaw's histrionic passion for Stella, which had sprung to life with

11

her casting for the lead and reached its climax when she fled from his importunities at Sandwich a few months before the play began. By then the actress was seeing herself in yet another role with the heir to a medieval castle as her adoring husband and a few days before the opening of *Pygmalion* she accepted that role and married George. It was thus that he got to know Shaw.

In his fifties he took to writing and published in the space of ten years a standard biography, two vintage books of memoirs, a popular book about dogs and three novels. He also had two plays performed and had written others, the interest of which lies today in their occasionally autobiographical flavour and in Shaw's detailed and diverting criticisms of them.

These criticisms, and other letters and messages written to him by Shaw are published here for, with three exceptions, the first time. They cover, with intervals, the period from the outbreak of the 1914 war, five months after Cornwallis-West's second marriage and the first performance of *Pygmalion,* until Stella's death in the spring of 1940. That event released her husband from the bond she had refused to break when their marriage was on the rocks, in spite of, perhaps even because of, Shaw's undertaking the thankless task of mediator in the private wars of these two people whom he knew very well indeed, better, probably, than they knew themselves. One is tempted to speculate on the play he might have made of the triangle of Jennie, Stella and George, with himself as intervener.

The letters shed yet more light on the characters of King Magnus and his Orinthia and on Shaw's kindness as a friend. Having written a lengthy criticism of one of Cornwallis-West's plays, he could not resist editing the original typescript so as to reduce the number of acts and writing into it a whole new scene.

The publication of the early volumes of Randolph

Churchill's biography of his father in 1966 brought the figure of George Cornwallis-West out of the shadows so far as his marriage to Winston's mother was concerned. Lady Randolph Churchill and Mrs Patrick Campbell both published their reminiscences, but their writings shed no light on the man who linked their lives or explain their determination to marry him. What manner of man was he to attract so strongly these two redoubtable women? What did they see in him? And what did he seek in them?

Even if the questions remain not wholly solved, it seemed to me, having known him well in his later years, that this third player in the trio should have his own story told. He was a man who with reason loved his father and feared his mother, a man of Celtic humour and melancholy, happiest in a setting of 'meadow, grove and stream', an affectionate rather than a sensual man, and one who loved acting a part, perhaps because he had been constrained to act one ever since childhood.

Various books reviving the story of Lady Randolph and her marriages have appeared since I began to write this book. For its purpose I have drawn on the memoirs of the three leading characters, on the Shaw-Campbell Correspondence, on the recollections of survivors in the village of Cornwallis-West's birth and on contemporary sources to furnish the Victorian and Edwardian backcloth against which the characters played their parts in the human comedy.

I 🌿 *Son and Heir*

'I must go into the city this morning,' George Cornwallis-West said one day, when he had settled on the research he required for his weekly column in *The Daily Telegraph,* 'the last of my father's Italian daughters has died and her settlement has to be cancelled.'

Cornwallis-West was born on 14 November 1874, at Ruthin Castle in Denbighshire, the event being precipitated — and this seems a key word for the confinement of many tough Victorian ladies — by his mother having chased the gardener round the grounds with a hosepipe in full spate. His grandmother, Lady Olivia FitzPatrick, finding the baby cast aside for dead by the midwife while she attended to the mother, successfully administered a slap and a nip of brandy to encourage his first cry.

Sixteen days later, on St Andrew's Day, another boy thrust his way into the world in an ante-room in Blenheim Palace, who was to play, among other, more spectacular roles, the role of George's stepson.

The announcement in *The Times* proudly described the Ruthin baby as 'a son and heir' for Major William Cornwallis-West, Lord Lieutenant of Denbighshire. He was baptised in the ancient parish church of St Peter, Ruthin.

William Cornwallis-West (he did not add a second Cornwallis and a hyphen to his name until 1886, and not by deed poll until 1895) was a great-grandson of the 2nd Earl De La Warr. Thomas, 2nd Baron West fought at Crécy and a La Warr daughter married a West after the families had vied at Poitiers for the capture of King John of France, whence they adopted as their motto *Jour de ma Vie*. More than two hundred years later it was Thomas West, 12th Baron De La Warr who, as Governor of Virginia, gave his name to the state of Delaware in the New World.

A fortress existed at Ruthin in the time of Edward I who granted it to John de Grey, Justiciar of Chester. In 1400 Owen Glyndwr stormed but failed to capture it; Henry VII somehow came by it, reputedly for a gambling debt. During the Civil War it was held for the king and after the Restoration was acquired by the Myddeltons of neighbouring Chirk, cousins of the Wests. Dr Johnson was taken by Mrs Thrale to see the 'very noble ruin' of Ruthin during their tour of North Wales in 1774, and they dined with another Myddelton family at Gwaynynog. 'Two tables were filled with company, not inelegant. After dinner the talk was of preserving the Welsh language' recorded the Doctor in his *Diary of a Journey into North Wales*.

In 1798 Sir Richard Myddelton's daughter, Maria, married as his second wife the Hon. Frederick West, a younger son of the 2nd Earl De La Warr. His elder daughter, Charlotte, was married to a Biddulph and a third, Harriet, was unmarried, and when he died he left no directions as to how his estates should be divided among them. They were apparently put in Chancery.

All were living together in Chirk Castle, the great fortress of twelfth century origin above the Dee, still lived in by Myddeltons today, and immediately a quarrel broke out between the two sons-in-law which lasted for years. It was the talk of the neighbourhood, and among the letters written to Mrs Maria West by those prolific letter writers, the Ladies of Llangollen, dubbed by Prince Pückler-Muskau 'the most celebrated virgins in Europe', there is one, hitherto unpublished, from Lady Eleanor Butler taking sides in

16

the strongest terms:

It is not by letter that our opinions of Mr Biddulph's extraordinary and outrageous conduct can be expressed . . . this last effort of expiring Malice will terminate in your complete triumph over an insane antagonist — for what but Insanity could dictate such a measure as he and his *Idiot* agent have adopted . . . we thought he attained to the very Acme of Meanness and Absurdity in the wretched business of the Grates — but he failed in his attempt to starve you to death as he will in his schemes to turn you out of your Father's House . . .

We have just had two Pies sent us from a great distance and we are anxious to have Mr Frederick West's assistance in carving them for the entertainment of his dear Parents, Aunt and Sister, as we should like to Carve Somebody if we could obtain a knife and fork of sufficient length and sharpness . . .

The reference in her second paragraph is to her friends' son, Frederick Richard, whom they had first met as 'a lovely little boy' in 1807. The Ladies rented some land for their flower garden from the Wests.

Eventually the suit reached the House of Lords, and when at length a decision was announced the families found themselves united at last in opposition to it. Having spent nearly a quarter of a million pounds on litigation, they summoned the village schoolmistress to supervise a draw for the three properties. The eldest daughter, Charlotte Biddulph, drew the longest straw and kept Chirk, Maria West drew Llanarmon, a shooting box, and some properties in the neighbourhood of Ruabon and Wrexham, and Harriet Ruthin Castle, and everyone was satisfied. Harriet, who remained unmarried, left Ruthin to her nephew, Frederick Richard West, by then an M.P., who installed an appreciative memorial tablet to her in the ancient parish church of St Peter. He mortgaged the estate and spent a great deal

17

of money on pulling down much of the existing fabric, which his parents had renovated, and rebuilding in red sandstone in the ancient style, incorporating some of the mediaeval walls and towers. A few years later George Borrow walked to Ruthin from Llangollen through the fertile Vale of Clwyd, guided by 'a poor weaver' who had never tasted duck until they dined on it together. He described the castle in *Wild Wales*:

Ruthin stands on a hill above the Clwyd... About three miles to the north is a range of lofty mountains dividing the shires of Denbigh from that of Flint, amongst which ... lifting its head high above the rest is the mighty Moel Vamagh, the mother heap which I had seen from Chester.

The original castle suffered terribly in the civil wars; it was held for wretched Charles and was nearly demolished by the cannon of Cromwell...The present castle is partly modern and partly ancient. It belongs to a family by the name of W—— who reside in the modern part and have the character of being kind, hospitable and intellectual people.

He explored the ancient part of the buildings:

... dark passages, a gloomy apartment in which Welsh kings and great people had occasionally been confined, that strange memorial of good old times, a drowning pit, and a large prison-room in the middle of which stood a singular-looking column... which had of yore been used for a whipping post.

Enough of the original structure remained, in fact, to provide a future generation of young Wests with the sport of letting playfellows get lost in the Plantagenet dungeons.

Many years before he acquired Ruthin Frederick Richard, when already the widower of one young heiress, had married another, Theresa Whitby, heiress of Admiral Cornwallis, whose story belongs in the next chapter.

Frederick and Theresa were, as Borrow had heard, highly

18

cultured people, and in order to pursue their artistic interests and rear a family out of range of the domestic feuds raging in the Welsh territories they had made themselves a second home in Italy, where numbers of the English and American intelligentsia congregated after the Napoleonic wars. By 1858 the American writer, Margaret Fuller, was referring to Florence as 'the Boston of Italy'. To mention but a few who lived or stayed in Florence during the Wests' long association with it, there were Lady Blessington, Leigh Hunt, Hazlitt; Trollopes, Thackerays, Brownings; 'Owen Meredith' the poet, later Earl Lytton, George Eliot (hence *Romola*), Frederick Tennyson; the Americans, Emerson, Nathaniel Hawthorne, Hiram Powers the sculptor, and their families, Harriet Beecher Stowe and Kate Field, young devotee of Walter Savage Landor, the doyen of them all. 'That quaint character Mr Kirkup' (Seymour Kirkup, artist) and in the early fifties the gifted psychic Daniel Dunglas Home, held *séances* which it was fashionable to attend.

In Florence, in March 1835, the Wests' second son, William Cornwallis was born and from his parents and his surroundings acquired a love of beauty from his earliest years. Having duly gone to Eton and been called to the Bar at Lincoln's Inn in 1862, he returned to pursue art and pleasure in the galleries of Florence and Rome, copying the old masters with remarkable skill and acquiring an Italian mistress and three daughters. He would have been happy to continue this idyllic mode of existence, but when he was thirty-three his elder brother died in Rome unmarried and it became incumbent on him to take up residence in Wales, administer the family estates comprising about 10,000 acres, and to produce an heir.

It took him another four years to sever his links with Italy, during which time he was appointed Lord Lieutenant and Custos Rotulorum of Denbighshire, Major of the Ad-

19

ministrative Battalion of Denbigh Rifle Volunteers and later Hon. Colonel of the 4th Bn. Royal Welch Fusiliers. Then, with an artist's eye rather than a lawyer's logic, he fell in love with the exquisite colouring and bewitching ways of the seventeen-year-old Mary Adelaide Virginia Thomasina Eupatoria FitzPatrick, daughter of Thomas 2nd Marquess of Headfort. 'A beautiful Irish savage,' was, unfortunately, how his mother saw her after her bad behaviour at a ball given in her honour, and his choice displeased his parents so much that they did not attend the wedding ceremony, performed by the Primate of Ireland, at St Patrick's Cathedral, Dublin, in October 1872; but he adored his wayward bride to the end of his life.

In response to an address of welcome from the tenantry when he took her home to Ruthin, he assured them:

The sunshine of her face will often gladden the cottage door, and I will undertake to say that the social duties she owes to other classes of society will not be omitted . . . the possession of property, rank or station in this life is attended by grave responsibilities.

He called her Patsy or, more intimately, 'Mussie'; she nicknamed him, for she became a great gardener, her Westaria Gigantia. Her favourite amusement in her new home proved to be that of sliding down the main staircase on a tea-tray.

Three children were born to William and Patsy by the time she was twenty-one: Mary Theresa Olivia, 'Dany' at home, known as 'Daisy' even in the formality of the German court circles where her destiny lay; Constance Edwina, 'Biddy' to her family and 'Shelagh' to friends and in her future role of Duchess of Westminster, and George Frederick Myddelton, who came between the two girls and was 'Buzzie' to them, and had a fate stranger than either of theirs in store.

While the children were small their parents decided to let

20

the Castle for a few years, hoping to repair their fortunes, which had suffered from the agricultural depression in Wales and from the spending in advance of rents which had not been collected because the tenants were too poor to pay them. Accordingly they removed to their London house at 49 Eaton Place.

A tall fair boy of four years old, dressed in a sailor suit and his elder sister's cast-off brown buttoned boots which 'hurt infernally', limping beside a perambulator containing a younger sister and pushed by a formidable nurse round Belgrave Square; or crossing Knightsbridge to the park in a state of terror because he has taken a piece of bread and jam which the nurse left on her breakfast plate and she has vowed to give him in charge to the policeman on point duty as a thief: these were among the earliest recollections of George Cornwallis-West.

Childhood humiliations are often remembered when pleasures have faded into oblivion, and he never forgot being dragged out of bed one evening to be takent o a fancy dress party. His sisters wore dresses they had had as bridesmaids and when asked what they represented were told to say 'Spring', but presumably for reasons of economy he had been put to bed instead of going with them. When they arrived, however, there were cries of 'Where's George?' from their hostess's daughters, so the carriage was sent back and George, dressed in the sailor suit that he wore every day, was taken to the party. Fifty years later he could hear the other boys asking him, with an undisguised sneer, what he was supposed to be, and a small voice answering 'A Jack Tar'.

The children of the aristocracy were not exempt from the rigours of Victorian childhood, dull food, stiff pinafores, tight boots, fear of misbehaving; nurses and governesses came and went in grim succession. On the other hand, Bolton the butler, who had been with their father

21

for years, was the young Wests' friend, and when there was a dinner party they would seat themselves in a window seat outside the dining-room 'like three sparrows on a perch' and be fed by him with choice morsels as the dishes were brought out.

The girls, who were adorably pretty, Daisy a little blonde and Shelagh a little brunette, were dressed up and taken out with their mother when she went driving in the park, one at a time because one child only in a carriage was the fashion. To quote Max Beerbohm, 'The modish appanage of Beauty in her barouche was not a spaniel now, but a little child'. Heads would turn to look at the beautiful young mother, the Prince of Wales would ride by and stop to speak and admire. Later, perhaps, he would call with *marrons glacés* and trinkets for the children and compliments for their witty mamma.

To Daisy his visits were remembered as being not entirely welcome, for they had to be thrust into best dresses and have their hair done at express speed as the Prince hated to be kept waiting; but when he put his hand in his pocket and produced, for instance, 'two little brooches like ladybirds' she and her sister were mollified. George was made happy by the fact that the Prince always asked to see him and never forgot him at Christmas.

The dinginess of his Victorian home, in common with that of other London houses, impressed itself on the small boy's memory. 'Gas, minus the mantle, was the only illuminant; coal fires and the appalling fogs of those days made everything grimy. The curtains, furniture and carpets were usually dark, as were wallpapers, because light colours would have made the dirt even more apparent.'

Sir Shane Leslie, who was to become Cornwallis-West's nephew by marriage, remembered the gloom of the interiors and the arrival, in his nursery in Seymour Street, of 'workmen who fumbled with wires'. When they had finished,

22

the blinds were drawn and he was told, 'Watch and you will see a new sun'. The miracle of electricity had been installed.

But there were those who preferred the older form of lighting. Ellen Terry and Henry Irving proudly used 'gas footlights and gas limes' at the Lyceum Theatre until they left it in 1902. 'The thick softness of gaslight,' wrote Ellen Terry, 'with the lovely specks and motes in it, so like *natural* light, gave illusion to many a scene which is now revealed in all its naked trashiness by electricity.'

Among the visitors to Eaton Place, Lord Charles Beresford, one of the famous trio of brothers renowned for merriment and mischief, was remembered as a distributor of shillings and half-crowns; and among the ladies, who flitted like gay parakeets among the dun draperies, were the popular beauties, Mrs Wheeler and Mrs Langtry, in their concertina bustles and little pork-pie hats decorated with silk pom-poms and their tippets of fur or feather. Patsy, their hostess, had a hat made of a ptarmigan sent her as a present by the Duke of Fife, the head jutting out in front, giving the impression when she wore it, of a bird sitting on a nest. Of her, a contemporary beauty, Lady Randolph Churchill, wrote that she 'held her own with the best of them. It was difficult to find a fault in her bright, sparkling face, as full of animation as her brown eyes were of Irish wit and fun. She had a lovely complexion, curly brown hair and a perfect figure'.

Mrs Langtry, the enchanting daughter of a Jersey clergyman, was married from the schoolroom to a widower whose main interest was yachting. Following an illness, London was surprisingly recommended for a change of air for the lovely young woman, and thither the Langtrys moved. After her first ball she became the rage. The Prince of Wales was charmed; her hair styles and her clothes were copied, distinguished men became her friends and she was painted by Millais holding a Jersey Lily, by Watts as the Dean's Daughter, and by Burne-Jones in various studies. Lady Randolph perceived the reason why: 'Artists extolled Mrs Langtry's classical Greek profile, golden hair and wonderful column-like throat, graced with the three *plis de Vénus*, which made her an ideal subject for their brushes and chisels'.

Whistler and Wilde were among her devoted slaves. Whistler came with a pot of gold paint and decorated the ceiling of her house in Norfolk Street. Wilde, who declared he would rather have discovered Lillie Langtry than have discovered America, brought Ruskin, who was not impressed by this artistry.

The Langtrys moved to Eaton Place, and in a letter quoted in Mrs Langtry's recollections Whistler sends an enclosure for Mrs Cornwallis-West, now a neighbour. No doubt she charmed the artist, but Patsy had acquired a reputation not only for beauty, and Mrs Langtry wrote generously of her attractions:

Mrs Cornwallis-West already the mother of three beautiful children, was petite with a vivid complexion, golden hair worn short. . . and flashing hazel eyes; equally attractive whether walking, on horseback or in a ballgown. She was high spirited, vivacious and extremely witty, sometimes audaciously so, and the possessor of a fine singing voice.

She had a characteristic story of a whirlwind visit from Patsy who, arriving from Ruthin without an evening dress, suddenly wished to go to the opera. Having succeeded in borrowing what the owner declared was, at the time, her one black dress, she went on from the opera to a ball, danced all night and next day returned the dress practically in rags.

It is difficult in our own day to envisage the interest and excitement created by uncommercialised beauty then,

24

especially when good looks were allied to intelligence and individuality. With her Irish charms and her ready wit, Patsy Cornwallis-West had a special advocate in the society versifier, Abraham Hayward, who, in the seventies 'old but active, flitted through the Victorian salons with a wide open eye and keen ear . . . and filled an important place in the literary world for forty years'. He it was who celebrated her charm and her talents, assisted by the Austro-Hungarian Ambassador of the day, in these verses:

To Mrs C.W.

who on being asked whether she was high or low church
said she was of no church

No church! then I too will have none –
No altar, no priest and no shrine;
All rites of religion I'll shun.
No *form* will I follow but thine.

When I kneel, it shall be at thy feet,
And I'll kneel till thou bid'st me to rise;
My role heaven shall be when we meet,
And I'll gaze on no stars but thine eyes.

To the Same

By the Austro-Hungarian Ambassador, Count Beust

Est ce *High* ou *Low*? quelle est donc son Eglise?
Les Hauts, les Bas, je les ai bien connus.
Ici, l'Incertitude n'est pas permise
Décidément par elle le Haut doit être cru.

Souvent au *High Church* on a reproché
De vouloir établir le culte des idoles,
Mais celle qui est elle-même idolâtrée
Ne peut, j'en suis certain, qu'y être dans son rôle.

25

Abraham Hayward summed up:

To Erin

Sure 'tis time now to give over sighing,
  When the bards of two empires compete —
When Albion and Austria are vying
  What tributes to lay at thy feet.

When that lovely young rebel is singing,
  Unfettered, the songs of her choice —
When the air all around her is ringing
  With the musical swell of her voice —

When the heart can scarce bear without aching
  The wild rush of emotion she wakes
And for *chains* she can't move without making
  A great many more than she breaks.

'Twill be some consolation to thee,
  After ages of sorrow and slaughter,
If no longer the land of the Free
  To know thou'rt avenged by thy daughter.

'Her passionate singing of "The Wearing o' the Green" would have aroused a revolutionary outburst in Ireland any day,' her daughter wrote, and Mr Gladstone, another admiring friend and Home Ruler, loved to hear her sing that song. For Laura Lady Troubridge 'Hers was the charm that enchains the heart and robs criticism of any wish to exercise its function. Her smiles began in her melting Irish eyes before they reached her full rosy lips'. It was only for her son that she had no smile, no outstretched arms.

According to Lady Randolph Churchill, a curious phase came over society at this time; 'so great was the licence allowed to the public that some ladies who had taken London by storm were publicly mentioned as "Professional

Beauties" . . . Invitations with "Do come: the P.B.s will be there" meant the certain attendance of society'. She herself was one. Mrs Cornwallis-West was another. Commercialism was creeping in and in 1879 Colonel Cornwallis-West was compelled to bring a libel action, occupying many columns in *The Times,* to scotch a vulgar canard in a popular magazine. It was to the effect that the backyard at 49 Eaton Place contained in each corner a small photographic studio into which after a lightning change of costume, his wife popped rapidly to satisfy the demands of photographers queueing for photographs of her to trade; and that later she drove round to the shops which displayed them, collecting commission. The offending writer received a sentence of six months' imprisonment, to run concurrently with one of eighteen months for libelling Mrs Langtry.

The 6th Duke of Portland in his memoirs, *Men, Women and Things,* had a story to cap all P.B. stories. Many years after the craze was over, he and his wife, after attending the Delhi Durbar, visited Egypt and went up the Nile to Luxor and Aswan where 'the donkey boys advertised the merits of their best animals by calling them, apparently irrespective of sex, "Mrs Langtry" and "Mrs West". When I asked about the others they said: "No! They no good — second class donkey. They only Antony and Cleopatra" '.

The men who were slaves to these beauties often had tremendous individuality and performed just for 'the hell of it,' feats which would now attract the widest publicity. Lord Desborough, Willie Grenfell to his friends, in the seventies ascended the Matterhorn three times, by different routes, and in the eighties swam the Niagara Falls, close in, not once but twice, the second time in a snowstorm with no 'fans' save an alarmed American lawyer from Buffalo who, having expressed doubts about the first swim, was invited to witness the second. Beside these exploits it is

27

almost an anticlimax to record that he won the school mile at Harrow in 4 minutes 37 seconds in 1874, stroked an eight in a clinker-built sliding-seat boat from Dover to Calais in 1885, sculled from Oxford to Putney, 105 miles, in one day, represented England in four international fencing competitions in the Olympic Games at Athens in 1906, and killed a hundred Scottish stags in one season.

Then there was Moreton Frewen, an outsize adventurer of ancient lineage who, almost accidentally, by following a buffalo train in deep snow over the Great Divide of the Rockies, accomplished a journey which, he realised only later, 'no man in all probability would ever attempt again — the passage of the main range of the Rockies from Camp Brown on the west, to Fort McKinney on the east, in December'. A year's cattle-driving in Wyoming and a two hundred mile walk along a prairie trail were nothing to him, who in 1881 transported his bride, Miss Clara Jerome of New York, with her French maid and her French trousseau, over these same two hundred miles in reverse, from the nearest railway point at Rock Creek to a pine-log house he had built on virgin prairie near Powder River. There had not, he assured her, been an Indian raid or a murder there since the previous year.

Somewhere in the background of all the social activity at Eaton Place Colonel Cornwallis-West had his studio, and artists, singers and musicians were among the friends who visited him there. His son remembered in particular Sir Francis Leighton and Sir John Millais, and a Welsh harpist who presented him with a violin at a tender age. The Colonel was immensely proud of his wife and loved to see her admired and enjoying herself; in his eyes she could do no wrong, but he did not share her appetite for society's amusements and preferred to live quietly behind the scenes with his painting and music, or meet his cronies in the Travellers' Club.

Occasionally he made an expedition to his shooting-box at Llanarmon in Dyffryn Ceiriog to canvass his tenants for their votes, and one such absence called forth a tender expression of concern from his elder daughter:

My dear old Poppets

I am thinking how dreadful it must be in the wild mountains among the Welsh people and I think I must write to you a little note to comfort you. I am taught that there are no roses without thorns, but I think the thorns for getting into Parliament must be very prickly ... Take care of your little self, dear old Dads, and come home soon to your little chickens who send you a lot of big kisses and hugs.

Your loving little daughter

Daisy.

Thus a seven-year-old in 1880. Her father did not win this particular election but represented West Denbighshire in Parliament as a Liberal from 1885 to 1892.

Eventually the family returned to Ruthin Castle after its long let, and nearly fifty years later Cornwallis-West described the excitement that welled up in him, whose only greensward had been London squares and parks, at the sight of the natural beauty which met his eyes as they approached the castle, escorted by the Mayor and Corporation and the town band. 'Never shall I forget my sensations when the great gates . . . rolled back and I found myself inside the grounds. It was a brilliant day; trees were just bursting into bloom. Their pale-green, the red-coloured sandstone of the castle and the blueness of the sky were in perfect harmony, and I felt I had arrived in fairyland.'

His father who 'loved every stone and every tree' of Ruthin, presented him to the tenants, at the rent audit dinner, as the Mab-y-castell, or heir to the castle, and to his delight one of them gave him a pony, which he named

29

May. Naturally the girls demanded ponies too, and so began the glorious gallops over the Welsh hills which were to make them all fearless riders.

The family passion for acting, that was to develop with the years, also manifested itself early when a Welsh nurse who was enlisted to act in tableaux was put in a bath, covered with a black shawl, her face floured, and told she was Marat, while Shelagh, as Charlotte Corday, stood over her with the biggest carving knife she could find.

But home was no fairyland. All should have been joy for these children with a young, high-spirited mother and a loving, tolerant father, and certainly Daisy remembered only the happy days, except when her nose was tweaked and her ears pulled to make her more beautiful; but because their mother was absorbed in her own exciting life and could not be bothered with them, they were left to the care of servants, except when she chose to vent some spite upon her son. Then, as he remembered more than forty years later, she personally locked him up in the dark cupboard under the stairs, deaf to his howls of misery and fear.

It was through her influence on his father, in whose eyes she could do no wrong, that George was sent not to a preparatory school with the sons of friends but to the Ruthin Grammar Free School, founded in 1595 by a native of Ruthin, Dr Gabriel Goodman, Dean of Westminster, for the instruction of boys born there. The local gentry also subscribed to its upkeep and on the list I saw of more or less illustrious names of those contributing at the time, the only one missing seemed, oddly enough, to be that of the Wests. George was given no pocket money. Naturally the local boys, expecting the squire's son to be well endowed, did not believe this, with the result that he was bullied or cajoled into buying sweets for them 'on tick'. A bill for tenpence-halfpenny, which he could not pay, was sent to the castle while his father was away, and was passed by his mother to the schoolmaster who, given *carte blanche* by her, administered a sound thrashing. He limped home, 'boiling with rage at the injustice', a pattern that was often to be repeated in his life, and Daisy rushed for the *Pomade Divine,* that universal salve, but there was no salve for wounded feelings.

True, his father once felt it his duty to chastise him, but he sent his son to choose the implement from the stick-heap. When it, not unnaturally, broke in his hand at the first contact, 'Dear, dear!' was all he said, 'What a pity! But there it is . . .' and that finished the episode.

The school buildings were pointed out to me with pride by John Edwards, an elderly man who had attended the school. 'My father kept the fish shop and he would give George a feed of shrimps whenever he had any to spare. He loved shrimps.'

'He used to come into the shop to borrow a pencil on his way to school and bring it back at night because he couldn't afford to buy one,' the stationer's daughter recalled. She could not have been as old as George, she said, when she told him he ought to wash his neck. One day she was invited to schoolroom tea at the castle and there was nothing to eat but bread and butter. 'Daisy wouldn't have cared, her head was always in the clouds and she wouldn't have known what she was eating, but Shelagh and George were furious. ' "Fancy! Visitors to tea and nothing but bread and butter!" and they rushed down to the kitchen and came back with some jam and a plate of strawberries that the staff were having for their own tea.'

In the late agent's house it was the same story. 'Father loved George,' said Mrs Forder, his daughter-in-law, 'and he loved father. When he was a boy he was always in and out of this house, more than at his own home, learning everything he could about wild life and fishing — and he

31

was always hungry, always ready for a feed, even after breakfast.'

'It was unheard of,' Cornwallis-West wrote many years later, 'for children to be allowed the same food as grown-ups. The only meal we had in the dining-room was lunch-eon, when special but entirely unappetising food was pre-pared for us. I remember my feelings at seeing and smelling the delicious-looking food offered to the more mature humans.'

The 9th Duke of Manchester in *My Candid Recollections* recalled that the usual fare provided for him and his sisters was a breakfast of porridge and milk, a midday dinner of bullock's heart and potatoes, and bread and milk for tea, their last meal of the day. One is reminded of Beatrix Potter who had a cutlet and rice pudding for her school-room dinner every day for years. No wonder little George burst into tears on being told by a governess that food would be unnecessary in heaven.

Even so, there were compensations. He caught his first trout at Ruthin on a May Day, with the aid of flies borrow-ed from Bolton, who was a keen angler, and an old rod of his father's mended with a bamboo stick from the carna-tions. Together they trailed through the parklands, casting a line in an occasional pool but with no luck until, under the bridge between Ruthin and Corwen, as the day began to cloud over, a very small fish obliged and he was able to present it to his delighted father that evening. The reward, five shillings and a new rod, and the discovery of an in-comparable solace for the misfortunes of the future.

His first ride to hounds was another unforgettable day. For reasons best known to herself, his mother condescend-ed to take him with her on his eighth birthday to a meet of the Vale of Clwyd Harriers. This was to be the real thing, not, as hitherto, with his pony being led 'like a dog' by a groom on a carriage horse, and he had visions of spectacular jumps mingled with a dread of falling off and disgracing himself. On the morning, however:

I had forgotten about the shabbiness of my saddle and had not even minded when my nurse called my gaiters 'buskins'! All I knew was that my pony had been sent on to the meet and that here I was in the brougham with my mother, setting out for the great event. I can see her now, with a tall hat tilted slightly over her forehead, on which she wore a fringe; a veil with large black spots, and habit of blue cloth buttoned down the front, with a tight waist and little tails behind. The skirt was of a newly invented safety pattern.

It was one of those magical days when everything surpassed expectation. May, the pony, jumped superbly, the Master congratulated him, a hare was killed and he was solemnly blooded and given a pad.

II 🌿 *Cygnet into Swan*

From 1886 George and his sisters had a third home where, free from the confines of London and the domestic rigours of Ruthin, they found themselves idyllicly happy; for the climate was mild, the grounds enchanting and the splendours of the New Forest all about them to challenge their prowess in riding.

In that year, their father inherited a life interest in the Cornwallis estates, entailed on his son, comprising some 2,000 acres in Hampshire which included the manor of Newlands, the dower house of Arnewood and the land and foreshore of Milford. Although the Colonel described the architecture of Newlands Manor as 'Churchwarden Gothic' and his daughter wrote of it as 'bad Strawberry Hill,' time and the 'velvety, sea-drenched air' had combined to make the place delightful.

The story of how it came into the family, and of how the name of Cornwallis came to be added to that of West, is a charming one. In the dining-room of Cornwallis-West's London home in the thirties there hung two portraits by Hoppner, the one of a superbly handsome young man in early 19th century naval uniform and powdered hair, the other of a beautiful and piquant young woman, with short dark curls, in a white directoire gown. They were of Captain John Whitby and his wife, Mary Anne Theresa Symonds, a wealthy sea-captain's daughter, and no one sitting at the table could fail to observe how strikingly their fine features and delicate colouring had been handed down to

34

their great grand-children, the host and his sisters.

While languishing in semi-retirement in Norfolk in the first year of his marriage, Nelson had written more than once to Admiral Cornwallis, brother of the 2nd Marquess Cornwallis, asking to serve under him in the East Indies command, but the latter replied that as Nelson's 'fireside was so totally changed' he had not ventured to name him for one of his ships. Eventually Nelson got a ship under Hood, and John Whitby served as his flag-lieutenant. Later Nelson reluctantly released him to Cornwallis, whose flag-captain he became.

In 1802, when Whitby married Miss Symonds, the bachelor Admiral invited the young couple to make their home with him at Newlands, the property he had bought a few years earlier. The existing house had been burned down and he was building a new one on the site.

Mary Anne Whitby, as well as being pleasing to look at, spoke several languages and painted 'exquisitely'. She was also, as it turned out, a shrewd business woman, and when the Admiral was recalled to sea as Commander-in-Chief of the Channel Fleet during Napoleon's threatened invasion, it was she who supervised the builders, laid out the grounds and plantations and managed the home farm in his absence. He vested her with the power of attorney and by judicious purchases of adjacent property she added considerably to the estate.

Her letters to the Admiral giving account of her stewardship were surprisingly free from the circumlocutions of the day. 'I hope to tell you Mitchel's farm is yours; negotiations have been set on foot on an entirely satisfactory basis,' she wrote, and did not neglect to mention matters of more domestic concern: 'We have got a little calf, a boy, the son of the old black and white Norman'. When her husband pressed her to take a holiday, 'I cannot leave Newlands,' she replied, 'the Admiral has set

35

me a task and I mean to complete it, pray God by the time you and he return'.*

In 1806 Cornwallis suffered a succession of blows. On the death of Pitt he was superseded in command by Lord St Vincent; his brother died suddenly in India, and John Whitby was sent home ill soon after being appointed to command H.M.S. *Ville de Paris,* and died also, leaving his widow with a baby daughter, Theresa John Cornwallis Whitby.

In deference to convention Mrs Whitby left Newlands, but the Admiral begged her to return. 'I have nothing to look forward to except a lonely old age,' he wrote, 'John is gone and you and your little dear have left me'.

Eventually she settled at Newlands for the remaining years of the Admiral's life, during which they travelled extensively at home and abroad as part of the child's education. He died in 1819, with her young daughter's hand in his, leaving her all his property in trust for Theresa and it was Theresa who in 1827 married Frederick Richard West and became the Cornwallis-West children's grandmother.

Their mother, Patsy, brought them up to think of her as an ogre. Of her erudite books of prose and poetry they knew nothing, though the mirth-provoking title of her three-volume novel, *The Doom of Doolandour,* dedicated to Elizabeth Duchess of Bedford, had penetrated to their ears. Neither did they know of her ardent support of Garibaldi, whom she had planned to welcome at Newlands, nor of her friendship with Browning and with Walter Savage Landor. She first met Landor in Wales at the house of his friend, Joseph Ablett, who had recently, in 1829, given him the Villa Gherardesca near Florence. Later he

*By a curious coincidence Admiral Cornwallis wrote to an old friend of his, Countess De La Warr, who happened to be staying near Newlands, asking her to call and befriend Mrs Whitby, which she did. He thus introduced to each other two ladies each of whom was to be his biographer's great-grandmother. G.F.M. Cornwallis-West, *The Life and Letters of Admiral Cornwallis,* Holden 1927.

used to stay with her and her husband in Hampshire and it was to her that his thoughts were to turn during his last years in Florence, when his brothers had refused him money for a favourite project, the preparation of his grave.

'I will beg my friend Mrs West to *give* me £10,' he wrote to Browning, and later, 'to this lady I have given my bust by Gibson and my daughter's by Bartholini. She would have been horrified to hear that my brothers should have refused me £10'. On her last visit to him he was too ill to see her, but one of his last acts was to send Browning a parcel for delivery to her in Florence, and after his death in 1864 verses were found in his desk* addressed to 'The Lady of Ruthin Castle' in acknowledgement of her composition 'Garibildi's March'.

There was a gap of twenty years in her writing, during which time she seems to have changed from the fluent composer of poetry and travel scenes and supporter of Italy's freedom, to the stern doyenne of the New Forest village where, after her husband's death in 1862, she 'reigned' in her mother's stead, castigating the vicar for his high church practices and writing stories for the Religious Tract Society with such titles as 'Owen's Fortune', 'Stella's Nosegay' and 'God's Arithmetic'. She had illustrated her earlier books with remarkably skilled woodcuts.

It remained to a future generation to destroy the bundles of letters Landor had written to her during a thirty years' friendship, because the only 'Landor' they knew of was a celebrated globe trotter and they could not imagine why their grandmother should have hoarded letters signed, as they supposed, by him. Possibly, as Edwardians, they imagined it to be more discreet to leave them unread than to investigate their contents.

Not long before she died, Grandmamma West relented sufficiently of her feud with her daughter-in-law to invite

*By Stephen Wheeler who published them in *Letters of Walter Savage Landor, Private and Public*, Duckworth, 1899.

George, on whom her property was entailed, to stay with her at Newlands. A dinner was arranged in honour of the shy eleven-year-old and his eating carefully supervised. Afterwards he was placed at a table to play draughts with a young lady while the other guests looked on. The next morning she consented to his fishing in the lake, accompanied by the butler, with a cord tied round his waist and fastened to a tree, humiliation to a seasoned fisherman. He never saw her again, but her memory was perpetuated for him, not as a dour old lady, but as a doe-eyed, smiling young woman in a picture hat drooping with features, her hands in a large ermine muff, whose miniature hung in his home.

In the benign atmosphere of Newlands the Cornwallis-West children spent what in after years seemed to have been the happiest time of their lives. Glorious gallops through the Forest, fishing in the narrow trout streams, or messing about in boats occupied their days. Their favourite game was circuses and their skill in bareback riding and in training their ponies and dogs to perform tricks earned for them from the Prince of Wales the nickname of 'The Wild West Show'. Indeed H.R.H. once addressed a telegram thus, which, with the destination 'New Forest', was safely delivered. Not unnaturally in their games George wanted to be the circus master and crack the whip, but the girls liked him to be the clown and they were two to one. Feminine domination was early established in his consciousness. An old neighbour of the Wests in Hampshire remembered arriving at a children's party at Newlands and finding his young host seated on a high stool with a dunce's cap on his head.

Shelagh, although the youngest, was the leader in their games and became a superb horsewoman. Comparing their two characters her sister wrote: 'Her stronger will and deeper nature are not for the shallow . . . Shelagh has great poise and self-control'.

38

At Newlands Patsy, who had a genius for such designs, made her elegant gardens, formal and wild, and here her husband pursued an architectural dream that was to materialise in after years as Milford-on-Sea. Here visiting royalty made an avenue of the trees they ceremonially planted (an occasional rusty metal label nostalgically remains) and here the children raced across the narrow bridge over the lake where the Prince of Wales fished for carp when spending as he liked to do, an informal weekend there after Cowes week; or through the grounds where their great-grandmother Whitby had planted a thousand dwarf mulberry trees, imported from Turin to nourish the silk-worms for her thriving silk-weaving industry in the village of Milford. By 1848 she was able to present the Queen with twenty yards of crimson and gold damask, and Mr Louis Schwabe, a Manchester silk merchant, having tested her wares, offered to take all she could produce, at 24s. a pound.

A fresh supply of funds having flowed into the family coffers as a result of Grandmama West's death, George eventually found himself at a preparatory school at Farnborough, where the savagery of the treatment was a hundred times worse than anything he had suffered at the hands of Ruthin boys or masters. Winston Churchill's description of the floggings at his own preparatory school corresponded so closely with Cornwallis-West's that it seems almost incredible that there were two fashionable and expensive schools – and probably more – treating their pupils with such identical savagery at this time, and that most parents, though not Winston's mother, turned a blind eye to it.

One summer his parents took a house at Southsea and he was invited by Princess Edward of Saxe-Weimar, whose husband was in command at Portsmouth, to go aboard a troopship with Prince Eddie and Prince George (the Duke of Clarence, who died, and his brother, who became George V), where their father, the Prince of Wales, was reviewing troops leaving for the first Boer War. The men were lined up on deck and he remembered being deeply impressed by the sight of a tear coursing down the cheek of an old soldier and wondering why he was crying. 'I had no knowledge then of the horrors of war', he recalled.

At last, in the liberal atmosphere of Eton, under the guidance of a universally loved tutor, Walter Durnford, the clouds of childhood began to lift. 'I felt as a prisoner must feel who has been released from a term of imprisonment. Life at Eton was to me a joy at all times.'

He began to develop his skill at cricket and shooting. During the holidays he learned to drive a locomotive on a quarry line on the Menai Straits, with practice on the foot-plate of the Bournemouth Belle, with a friendly engine driver. 'I would sneak onto the footplate at Basingstoke and ride on it, contrary to all regulations, as far as Brocken-hurst . . . good fellow that he was, he took a grave risk in teaching me. By the time I was twenty I knew all there was to know about a locomotive.'

Sometimes he stayed at Knole, where 'Cousin Lionel', the old Lord Sackville, encouraged his interest in the beautiful and historic objects that filled the house. In win-ter, when the family were at Eaton Place, he and his younger sister shared London's juvenile amusements, one of which was the Aquarium at Westminster, a sort of music-hall with side-shows, and a few perch or pike in a tank to justify its name. Here they could see Zazel, a woman, shot out of a cannon twice daily, or a man dive from the roof into a shallow tank. There were also Dr Kennedy, the Mesmerist, and Succi, the Fasting Man. Sir Charles Duff-Assheton-Smith once invited them to accom-pany him there, and on the way stopped the cab at a baker's and bought a bag of buns, which they sat munching steadily inside the Aquarium in front of the emaciated Succi, hoping to make his mouth water. Charlie Duff, when challenged on the ethics of the situation, replied with logic that it served the man right for making such an ass of himself.

Among the fashionable pastimes, bicycling in Battersea Park was all the rage, with the girl of the moment dressed in a flowing skirt and short jacket, a shirt blouse with stiff collar, a belt round a waspish waist and a small plate of straw on her head completing the outfit.

From Eton Cornwallis-West went to Freiburg in Baden to study languages, with a view to entering the diplomatic service. He spent a carefree time, fishing in the Black Forest, walking in the Vosges Mountains and mingling with the students, sometimes as the guest of a crack corps, when he witnessed some hair-raising duelling with sabres. Calf love, he found, was rampant.

The blonde beauty of Daisy in her first London season had captured the heart of Prince Hans Heinrich of Pless, heir to a wealthy family of ancient lineage and high rank at the German court, and some years older than herself. She was to have fabulous jewels, enormous castles, retainers galore and a husband whose generosity was boundless. All that was required on her part to marry into the House of Hochberg, the family name of Pless, was to produce sixteen armorial quarterings. As her father could trace his descent back to Henry III 'a thing like a patchwork quilt' arrived from the College of Heralds showing the lineage of the West-la Warr family from the thirteenth century onwards. Years later I saw it, bound in scarlet morocco and too heavy to lift, in a house in Ruthin, having been rescued from a scrap heap after the sale at the Castle.

Brother George came home to be an usher at the wedding, at St Margaret's, Westminster, and was given his first frock coat. Daisy wore a diamond coronet in the style of

41

a Countess of the Holy Roman Empire, which was now one of her titles. The Prince and Princess of Wales signed the register, the Cockney crowd as she left the church cried 'God Pless you!' Her last act as a member of the Wild West Show was, in her ignorance of fashion, to put on her smart French going-away dress back to front.

The following summer Cornwallis-West learned that, Sitwell-like, his parents had decided in his absence that he should not, in spite of his aptitude for languages, go into diplomacy but into the army. It was too late for him to enter Sandhurst, but his father, as Lord Lieutenant of Denbighshire, was able to give him a commission in the Third Battalion of the Royal Welch Fusiliers, and he spent a glorious winter at their Wrexham depot, hunting with Sir Watkin Wynn's hounds, before life became real and earnest.

Cramming for examinations followed at Jersey and Camberley. Three happy years slipped by, owning an old chestnut mare, making new friends, and learning to gamble at cards. From Camberley it was possible to catch a late train to London and still have plenty of time in town. Fancy dress balls at Covent Garden, which were attended by many stage beauties of the day and required only masks and dominoes from Clarkson's, were a favourite amusement with the young men. There were no night clubs, and the nearest approach to one, the Corinthian in St James's Square, petered out, apparently unable to compete with the attractions of the Empire promenade.

In 1895, having passed his examinations, in one of which he gained 90% for an essay on military music, he was gazetted to the Scots Guards and found life at Aldershot to his liking, though conversation in the mess did not rise above the subject of sport, and a well-intentioned kick on the shin from his neighbour foiled an attempt to discuss a religious festival at dinner.

From Aldershot the battalion went to Ireland, in those days the Mecca of all soldiers, for every kind of sport was obtainable, living was cheap and the people kind. These were carefree years, when drill in the Phoenix Park was not strenuous, when dogs accompanied their owners on route marches and when Company Orders could be done at 8 a.m. in full hunting kit before catching the special train to the meet. For race meetings within easy reach of Dublin, such as Leopardstown and Baldoyle, the battalion used its own four-in-hand, which the subalterns had to learn to drive.

Cornwallis-West had stayed in Ireland with his grand-mother FitzPatrick and loved the country and the appealing crankiness of its people. He understood their desire to please — that made a keeper say the bog was full of snipe when it wasn't — and the curious Celtic tempera-ment which, when they were not in the highest spirits, plunged them into the depths of despair. When he came to write his reminiscences they and their animals occupied three chapters.

Leave was sometimes spent with Daisy in the great palace of Pless where there was no bathroom until her husband had one made for her of gold mosaic. She has told in three books remarkable for their picture of a vanished European world how, with a bell being rung and a foot-man to precede her when she went from one room to another, the young girl fresh from the schoolroom and the forest games longed for her unconventional family. When her carriage drew up at Pless or at Furstenstein, a castle on the Silesian border, there was always a gorgeously-dressed man with a cocked hat and a tall silver staff which he flourished as he saluted, whom the FitzPatrick sense of the ridiculous goaded her into calling 'Guy Fawkes'. One even-ing she appeared at dinner in a dress she had made out of two new sacks from the stables, just 'to tease dear old Vater,' her father-in-law, who was Hans Heinrich XI, Duke of Pless, a *grand seigneur* of the old school.

Daisy grew to be fond of her German homes, especially beautiful Furstenstein, and in a diary entry in November 1896 she was torn between it and her longing to see them all at home, 'darling brother George and dear Newlands and the lovely sea'. She had not yet produced an heir, and tactfully she counts her blessings and thanks God for them before mentioning her petition for 'a little baby boy, please dear God'. She was to be rewarded with three sons.

George once had the honour of being invited to Promnitz in Prussian Silesia to shoot one of the only twelve stags which were allowed to be shot in a year and which were usually reserved for the Emperor, Crown Prince and other German princelings. Each stag cost between three and four hundred pounds. The stalk spread over four days and he distinguished himself by shooting two, one head winning first prize at the Sportsmen's Exhibition in Berlin that winter. He hunted boar and bison in the same forest, the Pless herd being by then the last bison in Europe outside Russia.

As late as 1924, when the first world war had swept away much of the past and when the Plesses had ended their marriage in the previous year, Lord D'Abernon, the British Ambassador to the new German republic, commented on the state that was still kept up at Furstenstein:

a fabulous castle belonging to Prince Pless, worthy of its reputation for size and luxury . . . Finely situated on an isolated hill dominating the plain and having, in the Middle Ages, formed the key to the frontier between Bohemia and Silesia. . . The prevailing note in decoration is German Louis XV, but a great deal of English comfort was added by his first wife, Princess Daisy, daughter of Mrs Cornwallis-West. The retainers, dependents and servants in the castle number about three hundred, without counting as many more at the Stud and in the

44

gardens. All household details are extraordinarily well organised — magnificent liveries, an English butler, numerous footmen in powder, a chasseur in top boots and uniform who stands behind the Prince's chair, and a police dog, reputed to be very savage, constantly at his heel.

'Personally,' added the English lord, 'I find it irksome to have two servants perpetually at my door. Magnificence should be reserved for rare — very rare — occasions.'

In May 1896 Cornwallis-West was given leave to go to Ruthin for his coming-of-age celebrations which had been postponed while he studied for his examinations. The house was full of visitors, balls and presentations had been arranged, but at the eleventh hour he was taken ill with quinsy and could attend none of the functions. To him it seemed ominous, and he had a foreboding that he would never live in the Castle as his father's successor.

It was with reluctance that he left Ireland when the battalion returned to Wellington Barracks in May 1897, but there were compensations. He was promoted and transferred to the 1st Battalion of his regiment, and found himself quartered in the Tower of London, and taking part not only in the ancient ceremony of the Queen's Keys but in Her Majesty's Diamond Jubilee.

The Gay Nineties were reaching their climax. Consuelo (née Vanderbilt) 9th Duchess of Marlborough, looking back, felt that in no other capital in Europe was there anything to equal the brilliance of the London season. She and her friends could be seen in the morning in the Row, wearing classic habits and riding thoroughbred hacks; in the afternoon at Ranelagh, the eighteenth century resort of fashion now resuscitated, or at Roehampton or Hurlingham watching the polo, and at early evening in the Park again, now in ruffles and lace, in their barouches. At

45

night the great houses formed ideal settings for magnificent entertainment.

The strange thing was that not only the Mayfair crossing-sweepers, who did well out of it, but the majority of the lower orders seemed to enjoy the spectacle, or at least the legend of opulence and idleness, rather than to resent it, and had their favourites among the dandies and the lovely ladies, whose names sometimes appeared in popular songs.

On the stage that season, the two great French actresses, Mme Sarah Bernhardt and Mme Réjane, were both playing in *Frou-Frou,* the one at the Adelphi and the other at the Lyric Theatre.

In the publishing world the anniversary year was commemorated by a revival of *The Book of Beauty,* the original of which appeared in 1841, when it was edited by the Countess of Blessington. The 1897 production contained a collection of portraits of leading beauties, embellished with literary and artistic contributions by some of them. A drawing of Lady Randolph Churchill, with diamond hair-prong, was among those by the talented Marchioness of Granby, better known as Violet Duchess of Rutland. The famous beauty, Mrs Cornwallis-West, hair piled high, profile perfect with its small patrician nose and short upper lip, was framed by two neatly-turned verses in her honour; her exquisite elder daughter, in her favourite cloud of tulle, contributed a page and a half on Happiness. Nearly all the beauties here are soulful, radiant, statuesque.

'It was not only an age of lovely women,' Dame Nellie Melba reflected when she was old,

It was a spacious age, when hospitality was far more lavish than it would ever be again. Who today, for example, would give a dinner-party in which there was a pearl in every soup-plate? . . . Some of those nights were indeed Arabian nights.

Most lavish of all, however, were the great balls . . .
at Stafford House, where Millicent Sutherland used to
look so superbly beautiful . . . at Devonshire House,
where the staircases were massed with orchids . . .
where the whole of the great families of Europe seemed
to be gathered together — Bourbons, Marlboroughs,
Romanoffs, Rothschilds — in one immense procession
of magnificence.

Allowing a little for the intoxication of a young woman
who had been brought up in a strict household 'down
under,' where, as she said, frugality was the order of the
day, her superlatives are confirmed by the reminiscences
of her contemporaries. The magnificence culminated in
the Diamond Jubilee celebrations.

The Queen, the fashionable journal of the day, announced in its column 'The Upper Ten Thousand' that Colonel
Cornwallis-West, Lord Lieutenant of Denbighshire and
Lord of the Manor of Ruthin, was presenting to the
borough of Ruthin a recreation ground in commemoration
of the occasion, and at the beginning of the day, 22 June
1897, his son found himself stationed on Ludgate Hill
where the Scots Guards were lining the route for Queen
Victoria's arrival at St Paul's Cathedral for the Thanks-
giving Service. He was duly impressed by that dignified,
diminutive figure. After the service Her Majesty travelled
to Aldershot in her new train, to review colonial troops,
blocks of ice concealed by ferns and damask roses being
placed in the carriage to temper the heat of the day.
That night, Cornwallis-West and some brother officers,
having dined with their commanding officer at Pirbright,
climbed to the top of the Nore and watched the lighting
of the beacon fires for miles around the countryside.

There followed a fever of social activity, a flurry of
balls, and at the most magnificent of them all, the fancy
dress ball at Devonshire House, he allowed himself to be

47

pressed into service in Daisy's entourage with the bribe of a free costume. She planned to go as the Queen of Sheba, with two girls and several men in attendance.

The 'inner circle of society,' in the phrase of *The Times,* organised itself into groups, some representing the royal courts of Europe, others those of the Orient, each headed by its female ruler. The hostess, the Duchess of Devonshire, went as Queen Zenobia. There were, regrettably, two Queens of Sheba, but the paper honoured the Princess with a detailed description of her robe of gold encrusted with immense turquoises, diamonds and other precious stones, jewelled girdle and, on her head, a bird of paradise and a crown: 'and four niggers held her train'.

Despite the magnificence of the electrically-lit gardens, the enormous banks of flowers, the hanging tapestries (at Grosvenor House the previous week the supper tent had been *carpeted* with Gobelin tapestries specially woven for the occasion), the groaning supper-tables and the rich apparel of the guests, young Cornwallis-West had a frustrating evening, for, he complained, with his blackened face and bizarre robe, his girl friends did not appreciate him, and he left early with rage in his heart against the famous designer of the set piece.

One pair of bright eyes seems, however, to have observed this slave's noble bearing despite his gaudy drapery, and discerned his fine features beneath the burnt cork. Sitting at the first supper table with the Prince of Wales and other royal guests, the widowed Lady Randolph Churchill, gorgeously attired as the Empress Theodora of Byzantium, noted that 'the Princess of Pless was surrounded by a retinue in oriental garb, some of whom had so far sacrificed their appearance as to darken their faces'.

Riding rather than dancing was his particular joy, and his cup of happiness seemed full when he managed to fulfil his ambition to win the Army point-to-point with a horse named Oxhill, later following it up on the same mount with the Warwickshire point-to-point, the Regimental Race and the Household Brigade Welter Steeplechase.

One day in the summer of 1898, while he was on a musketry course at Hythe, he was surprised to receive an invitation from the Countess of Warwick to spend a weekend at Warwick Castle where the Prince of Wales would be on a visit. Normally leave from the course was unlikely to be granted; on the other hand an invitation to meet the Prince amounted almost to a command. He saw his Colonel, Ian Hamilton, explained the position, and was given leave.

One may wonder how he came to be chosen to receive an invitation to a party consisting mainly of older people in the Prince's set and, at this distance of time, may suspect that either Frances Warwick was amusing herself with a little game of her own, or that she was obliging her friend. In any case, the visit was a fateful one, for on arrival he was introduced to Lady Randolph and was struck by her youthful appearance and her charm and vitality. They went on the river together in the beautiful setting afforded by the Castle, and immediately became friends.

III ❧ Jennie

The remarkable woman who had come into George Cornwallis-West's life was the second of the three surviving daughters of Leonard Jerome, an American of Huguenot origin, who worked his way from his farmhouse near Syracuse, in Western New York State, to the top of several worlds; and of his wife, Clara Hall, a dark shy beauty with, it was said, a dash of Iroquois blood in her veins, whose life was devoted to grooming her daughters for stardom, in accomplishments as well as style, in the leading society of Europe.

Jennie Jerome, born in Brooklyn, brought up in Paris, strikingly beautiful, and blessed with a father whose *métier* was making fortunes on Wall Street, had a gay, extrovert nature and a powerful personality. She radiated energy and a passion for living. Life was her cornucopia from which all that was fine and beautiful must flow at her whim. Dresses from Worth, diamonds from Cartier, piano duets with Paderewski, princes and prime ministers her guests: these were the standards she accepted as her right. Money, for her, had no meaning: if one source ran dry there were others to be tapped.

Her father at one time virtually possessed 'the whole of the Pacific Mail Line. . . For a short period he was co-editor of the *New York Times*. . . He founded Jerome Park and the Coney Island Jockey Club, the first of the two great American race courses and. . . made good his claim to be called "the father of the American turf" '.

That was almost all his daughter said about him when she came to write her reminiscences. For his family he was mainly a beloved money-spinner. It was left to a great-granddaughter to write the whole story of this many-sided man of colossal energy and enterprise, who made and lost fortunes, went buffalo-hunting on the Western Plains when he was bored, adored yachts of ocean-racing calibre, and horses and music and pretty woman, and either launched or enhanced the careers of at least four celebrated singers, including Jenny Lind and Adelina Patti. One of his protegées was the lovely Mrs Ronalds, an American of good family, credited, or rather debited, with dubious adventures in Paris and elsewhere, who starred at his Jerome Theatre in his private opera company, gave gorgeous presents to his children (and accepted some from their father) and finally settled in London, with a musical salon and a box at the opera. Jennie was the second of his three daughters; a fourth, Camille, had died in early childhood. Her elder sister, Clara, named after her mother, eventually became Mrs Moreton Frewen. The younger, Leonie, was to marry Jack Leslie, son and heir of Sir John Leslie, Bt, of Castle Leslie, Glaslough, in Co. Monaghan.

Jennie wove into her reminiscences the story of a babyhood spent in Trieste, where her father, who went there as American consul, with his young family, in 1852, sailed his first yacht and drove a pair of high-stepping horses from the Austrian Imperial Stud; but in fact she was born in Brooklyn in 1854. Even so, her real memory, apart from the talk about Trieste that she may have absorbed into her mental vision as a child, stretched from the American Civil War, when every little Southerner met at dancing class was 'a wicked rebel' to be pinched if opportunity offered; to the funeral of Abraham Lincoln when her home in Madison Square was draped in black and white

51

and the whole city looked like a 'gigantic mausoleum'; to hours of intensive pianoforte tuition, with the prospect of becoming a professional musician; to the glamour of Paris towards the end of the Second Empire, when 'never had the Empire seemed more assured, the Court more brilliant, the fêtes more gorgeous', and to her escape with her mother and sisters Clara and Leonie from their fine house on the Boulevard Haussman, just before the Prussians entered Paris in 1871, to Deauville, and soon afterwards to London and Brown's Hotel.

That summer they spent happily at the Villa Rosetta at Cowes, and returned to it in 1873. The yachting season was passed among the English royalty and nobility at their most informal. The dazzling good looks of the elder girls (the youngest was now at school in Germany) and their professional playing of duets, in contrast with the often insipid performances of English young ladies at parties, inevitably distinguished them in any gathering. And were they not dressed by Worth?

Almost immediately the pattern of Jennie's future life was shaped for her. At the Royal Naval Squadron Ball in August 1873 she was presented to the Prince of Wales, an important contact which was to stand her in good stead, and at a dance given on the cruiser *Ariadne* in honour of the Czarevitch and Czarevna of Russia she met Lord Randolph Churchill, the younger son of the seventh Duke of Marlborough. Their falling in love at first sight has passed into history.

Within three days he had told his love and found it returned. They rushed to inform their parents of the news, demanding instant marriage. The Marlboroughs were appalled: they could not conceive what sort of family their son had taken up with. Mrs Jerome would not hear of it and removed her daughters to Paris out of harm's way. Only Mr Jerome, getting the news tardily in New York, at first looked kindly on Jennie's obvious happiness and approved her choice of an Englishman, but revolted when he heard of the Marlboroughs' reluctance to receive his cherished child into their family.

Negotiations were prickly and to the impatient lovers painfully protracted. In the midst of private turmoil a General Election might have passed almost unnoticed by them, but the Duke made it a condition of his son's marrying that he should first enter Parliament. Fortunately the dissolution of Gladstone's government early in 1874 gave Lord Randolph his opportunity; he stood as Tory candidate for the Borough of Woodstock and was elected.

'There is nothing more to be done except to pay the bill, and that I have left to my father.' Although this was written to his fiancée about the expenses of the election campaign it might well serve, with slight variations, as the guiding principle of all the leading characters in this story. So pleased, however, was the Duke with the result of the election that he withdrew his objections to his son's marriage and travelled to Paris to meet the lady's parents. The meeting was a success, and in the bride-to-be's view 'all that Papa need now do' was give her a large dowry and the wedding could take place.

Leonard Jerome, most generous of men, found himself in a dilemma, for the American laws relating to the rights and status of married women were very different from the English ones, which denied a married woman any entitlement of her own money. Moreover, in his code, a man should be ready and able to support the woman he meant to marry.

Again there was brief turmoil. All the protagonists being fluent letter-writers, hundreds of words were exchanged. Randolph heroically declared he would earn his own living. This threat, coupled with Jennie's tenacity, soon put an end to parental bargaining. Mr Jerome made a liberal settlement; the Duke, who was also a devoted father, paid all his son's creditors and provided him with an income. On 15 April 1874 Jennie and Randolph were married at the British Embassy in Paris, amid a flurry of satin and lace and maternal tears and bridal smiles. The future seemed set fair.

They returned from a brief continental honeymoon to Blenheim to be welcomed by the cheering tenantry, and by the Duke and Duchess to their vast home. Before long the formality of the Palace household, where old-fashioned state was kept up, began to be oppressive to the American girl, whose only experience of English life apart from Brown's Hotel, had been the *dolce vita* of Cowes. She found the quietness and tedium hard to bear. Her days were spent in reading the newspapers in order to talk knowledgeably at the dinner table, in practising the piano with a skill acquired from the best masters that Jerome money could obtain, and in changing her costume before, apparently, every meal. A drive or a visit might occupy the afternoon and a game of whist the evening, until on the stroke of eleven one could take up one's candle, kiss the Duke and Duchess goodnight, and thankfully seek one's bed.

Joyfully she escaped with her husband to their first home, a furnished house in Curzon Street, to enjoy the delights of the London season as a married woman. Her beauty took London by storm and they soon found themselves drawn into the exclusive Marlborough House set of the Prince and Princess of Wales. Vividly she recorded, years later, the whirl of gaieties and excitements, of balls lasting till dawn, of dinners, plays and parties, and not least the classic race meetings they attended, for Randolph loved the turf and gambling was in his wife's blood.

In the autumn there was shooting and hunting at Blenheim and, prematurely, as *The Times* announced, an event

54

occurred there which she did not trouble to mention in her reminiscences. On St Andrew's Day, 30 November 1874, she gave birth to a son whose entry into the world would not be delayed, even though his baby clothes were not ready for him. He was christened Winston Leonard Spencer Churchill and was put away in his nursery in the larger London house to which his parents now moved, in Charles Street, where they could entertain the Prince and Princess of Wales and Lord Rosebery and Mr Disraeli. The Jeromes came over to see their first grandchild and Clara spent the season with her sister, vetting the young men Jennie produced for her approval.

Randolph had delivered his maiden speech in Parliament not long after they were married, when Disraeli had reported to the Queen that it showed great promise, and had since then made his presence felt in the House. Apart from murmurs of money shortage to Papa, a kind of perpetual 'noises off', it was a time of bountiful hope.

All the more shattering, therefore, was the *débâcle* when Lord Randolph had the misfortune to offend the Prince of Wales by championing his elder brother, the Marquess of Blandford, in the affair known as the Aylesford scandal, in which the Prince took the opposite side and himself became implicated. Lord Randolph threatened his exposure, a duel was mooted, the Prince told the Queen, the Cabinet became involved.

As a result the Churchills found themselves literally out of court and barred from any house where the Prince visited lest H.R.H. should boycott it, and the long-suffering Duke of Marlborough now accepted, under pressure from Disraeli, the office of Viceroy of Ireland. Randolph, it was agreed, should act as his unpaid private secretary. On 12 December 1876 the Duke, accompanied by his son, arrived in Dublin, on a bitterly cold morning as the *Annual Register* noted, to be sworn in and attend various ceremonies, and

55

on 10 January 1877 he returned to make his 'grand public entry', accompanied by the Duchess and all his family and retinue, in procession to Dublin Castle. They took up residence in the Viceregal Lodge, with Randolph and Jennie and toddler Winston close by, in the house of the official Private Secretary, Captain Percy Bernard, by a friendly arrangement.

A much quoted but indispensable picture of young Lady Randolph at this time appears in Lord D'Abernon's *Portraits and Appreciations:*

> I have the clearest recollection of seeing her for the first time . . . at the Vice-Regal Lodge . . . The Viceroy was on a dais at the farther end of the room . . . but eyes were not turned on him or his consort, but on a dark, lithe figure standing somewhat apart . . . radiant, translucent, intense. A diamond star in her hair — her favourite ornament — its lustre dimmed by the flashing glory of her eyes. More of the panther than the woman in her look, but with a cultivated intelligence unknown to the jungle. Her courage not less than that of her husband — fit mother for the descendants of the great Duke. . . With all these attributes of brilliancy, such kindliness and high spirits that she was universally popular. Her . . . delight in life and the genuine wish that all should share her generous faith in it, made her the centre of a devoted circle.

In Ireland she and Randolph were able to indulge to the full their passion for hunting, Jennie taking tosses with fortitude. When the failure of the potato crop precipitated the famine of 1879, they travelled round the country and saw for themselves the abysmal conditions of the poor. Randolph became secretary to his mother the Vicereine's Irish Relief Fund, and his wife gained experience in the organising of money-raising efforts, for which she was later to become famous.

'The heart-rending poverty of the peasantry in their wretched mud-hovels' remained in her memory for the rest of her days, and in their son Winston's view the Irish experience 'altered, darkened and strengthened' his father's life and character. Without it, he felt, 'he would never probably have developed popular sympathies or the courage to champion democratic causes'.

Their exile lasted three years. In 1880 a General Election, in which Disraeli was defeated by Gladstone, brought to an end the Duke of Marlborough's term of office as Viceroy, and the Randolph Churchills found themselves back in England with another house, in St James's Place, and a new son, John. Jennie was developing her flair which became quite famous among her friends, for furnishing and decorating houses, but now learned to her cost that expensive silk panels used for drawing-room drapery could be ruined by London fog.

Still debarred from Marlborough House, but realising that her husband's political star was in the ascendant as a result of his disturbing speeches in the House of Commons and elsewhere on the subject of Ireland, she took to visiting the House to listen to debates. The political scene fascinated her. She found Lord Salisbury and Mr Gladstone pleasant companions, enjoyed a passage of arms with Sir Charles Dilke and Mr Chamberlain, and was assured by Lord Goschen that her conversation interested him so much there was not a woman in London he liked more to take into dinner.

There is another arresting description of her in these years in the memoirs of Laura Lady Troubridge.

At Reigate Priory, the home of Lady Henry Somerset, Lady Randolph Churchill . . . wore . . . a simple white dress, high but transparent enough to show the marvellous line of her neck and shoulders. She was gay and full of the zest of life, and after dinner she sat down at the piano and played and sang her American songs in a full, rich voice. 'Razors a-flying in the air' was one of them, and several Negro spirituals. The white dress, the Castilian darkness of her colouring, the dim background, all made up a vision to me.

Her husband matched her for style. He wore colourful clothes and conspicuous jewellery. 'The newspapers were filled with his portraits and doings,' Lady Dorothy Nevill remembered, 'whilst his twirling moustache proved a never-ending subject of amusement to the caricaturists. Theatres and music-halls rang with references to "Randy-Pandy" '.

In July 1883 Randolph's father, the 7th Duke of Marlborough, suddenly died. Randolph and Jennie had to wait another three years before the breach with the Prince was healed. To mark the reconciliation he and the Princess dined with them in what was to be their last new home, 2 Connaught Place, overlooking Marble Arch, where warned by experience, they chose a modern décor of panelling and white paint.

Jennie's interest in politics was stimulated by the formation of the Primrose League by her husband and three of his friends in November 1883. Its objects were the maintenance of Religion, of the Estates of the Realm, and of the Unity and ascendancy of the Empire, all burning questions of the day. A Ladies' Grand Council, with the Duchess of Marlborough, the Marchioness of Salisbury and the Countess of Iddesleigh as its Presidents, was formed in 1884, and as a Vice-President Jennie travelled the country inaugurating new Habitations, as the branches were called. 'Politics, like charity, is a great leveller,' she decided, when 'the labourer and the local magnate, county lady and grocer's wife' trooped up to sign the roll.

She was again to find it so when in 1885 Lord Randolph was appointed Secretary of State for India and, on accepting office, was obliged to seek re-election in his constituency.

He knew by now that he could confidently delegate her to organise the campaign in Woodstock to fight the Liberal candidate, and with his sister, Lady Georgiana Curzon, she set up Tory headquarters at the Bear Hotel, whence, in a tandem drawn by horses decorated with Randolph's racing colours, they drove round the countryside appealing prettily for support. Needless to say, the seat was retained, and to Jennie returning to London with the sweet smell of success in her nostrils, it seemed odd that the crowds in the city streets did not recognise and applaud her.

She took a now familiar part in helping the Vicereine of India, Lady Dufferin, to raise money for her fund for supplying medical aid to the women of India, and in due course received the Order of the Crown of India at the hands of the Queen with the same ingenuous pleasure that her son later showed in tokens of merit.

The Primrose League, meanwhile, had attracted the attention of the formidable Lady Paget. Born Countess Walburga von Hohenthal, she was the wife of Sir Augustus Paget, British Ambassador first in Rome and from 1884 to 1893 in Vienna, and was, with her voluminous diaries, the Boswell of half Europe. While visiting the Salisburys at Hatfield House in 1886, when Lord Salisbury was Prime Minister, she took the first opportunity to make the onslaught she had, as she put it, hatched.

This Primrose League has become a great power in the land, but having begun as a half-joke it is like a child that has outgrown its clothes and is terribly badly managed at headquarters . . . I therefore took it upon myself to speak to Lady Salisbury . . . We concerted an altogether new departure. . .

The same evening she examined Lord Salisbury's palm and was struck by 'his unequalled logic, but the power in these lines is a little too much governed by affection and natural courtesy. He ought not . . . ever to give way to

59

anybody else's opinions'.

In July that year, under Lord Salisbury's renewed premiership, Randolph Churchill was made Chancellor of the Exchequer and Leader of the House of Commons. Excitement welled up in Jennie's heart, for she and his friends could not but believe that these appointments would lead eventually to the highest office.

Lady Paget sketched a lively picture of him that autumn:

Lord Randolph came in. The worn, middle-aged man with the heavy tawny moustache hardly recalled to me the smooth-faced, dark-haired stripling, I remembered . . . Only the rolling eyes, set in orbits like saucers, and the turned-up nose remained. The shyness and the silence was gone. But the insistence and at times impertinence of manner was still there, accompanied by strong, *saccadé* gestures. He was . . . clever and quick with enormous 'go' . . . It is this 'go' that I fear, for it takes a gentle, thoughtful nature like Lord Salisbury's by storm. There is something most catching about animal spirits, perhaps the more so when contained in so slender and odd-looking a vessel as Lord Randolph.

She might have spared her fears for the gentle Lord Salisbury, for within a few months Randolph had achieved his own political destruction.

Winston Churchill has described in detail the events leading up to the crisis in his father's career. In brief, he crossed swords in the Cabinet over his budget of December 1886, the point at issue being the treasury allocations for naval and military expenditure and, unable by nature to make concessions, wrote a letter of resignation to the Prime Minister, on Windsor Castle writing paper, while on a visit to the Queen. To her he did not mention his action, although he informed *The Times*. Lord Salisbury appeared to accept it with alacrity. Not only the Queen but his

60

wife read the news in the morning paper. She came down to breakfast with 'the fatal paper' in her hand, to find her husband 'calm and smiling'. 'Quite a surprise for you' was his only comment. It must have bitten deeply for her to have recreated the scene in her memoirs. It was Christmas time and the boys were home.

The thunderclap of Randolph's resignation put every-thing else in the shade. Devotedly ambitious for him, Jennie realised that he had signed his political death warrant. 'The political world stood aghast, every hand seemed against him . . . It was gall and wormwood to me to hear Randolph accused in every quarter.' She had felt so certain that he would enjoy the fruits of office for years to come and, practical woman that she was, she 'regretted these same fruits'.

Margot Asquith, seeing Jennie for the first time at Punchestown Races a few months later, made a characteris-tically caustic note: '. . . a woman in a Black Watch tartan skirt, braided coat and astrachan hussar's cap. She had a forehead like a panther's and great wild eyes that looked through you . . . Had Lady Randolph Churchill been like her face, she could have governed the world'. Could Lord d'Abernon have filched, unconsciously, the symbol of the panther for his famous portrait, or was it a question of two minds finding independently *le mot juste*?

At the end of 1887 they visited Russia and again the acid Paget pen recorded in January 1888: 'Randolph Churchill is doing all the mischief he can in St Petersburg. The Emperor told me that everyone was enchanted with him there. He and the Russians spend their time in mutual *enguirlandage*'. Doubtless they were also enchanted with his wife, who later wrote a fascinating description of life in St Petersburg and Moscow at that time.

They arrived home to find *The Times* devoting three columns to their visit to Russia in spite of the fact that

Churchill was no longer in a position of power. Jennie, dining with the Prime Minister and finding him unwilling to speak of her husband, formed the impression that they would never be reconciled. Sadly she admitted to her sister Leonie:

> I feel very sick at heart sometimes; it was such a splendid position to throw away. In the bottom of my heart, I sometimes think that his head was quite turned at that moment and that he thought he could do *anything*. However it is an ill wind that blows *no* good and R. has been so much easier and nicer since that I ought not to regret the crisis. . .

Debts had mounted more than ordinarily and in 1891 Randolph went off to South Africa in search of 'sport, gold and health'. The first two objectives were attained, the gold in the shape of rapidly rising Rand shares, sufficing ironically to settle his posthumous debts: the third was not. His health was visibly deteriorating, though he himself was the last person to realise it and continued to address, with speech and movement impaired, an embarrassed House. As is now well known he had for years suffered from an incurable form of venereal disease affecting the central nervous system, which increasingly weakened his mental and physical powers. With the intimations of the illness that was to warp his mind and eventually kill him, a bitter change had come over Jennie's husband. The marriage went irretrievably wrong and she had had to make her own life and find elsewhere the joy and affection that her nature demanded, but she remained loyal to her husband and devoted to her sons.

In 1894, against medical advice, they began their much publicised world tour, planned to take in Canada, Japan, China, India and Burma. On it his wife's courage was to be tested to the utmost limit. In Sir Shane Leslie's words, 'She attended him to dinners where in his speech he was liable to substitute well-known truths for conventional courtesies, and she cheerfully crossed the tropical seas though it was necessary to include a leaden casket among their baggage'.

Inevitably Lady Paget, when news of Randolph's failing health began to circulate, had been passing on the court gossip that after his death his widow would marry Count Charles Kinsky, the handsome Austrian popular in London society, who had for years been the chief among her lovers, 'which won't be very pleasing to his family'.

There is a glimpse of Kinsky as a larger-than-life figure at a wine-tasting party in the Prussian imperial cellars; he appears in Winston's boyhood as a great giver of treats; and in the stables at Glaslough, their Irish home, the Leslies found a saddle he had had made for Jennie 'after he won the Grand National on Zoëdone in 1883 no one thought an Austrian could', according to the label on it.

Now, at Rangoon, in the midst of her trouble, she received a telegram telling her of his engagement.

'I *hate* it,' she cried, in an unburdening letter to Clara. 'I shall return home without a friend in the world and too old to make any more'.

They were continuing their journey into India when Randolph collapsed at Madras and they were compelled to return to London.

From 50 Grosvenor Square where for the sake of economy they now lived with his mother, she wrote to Leonie, who had evidently offered to come and comfort her over the Kinsky affair: 'The bitterness, if there was any, has absolutely left me. He and I have parted the best of friends and in a truly *fin-de-siècle* manner . . . He has not behaved particularly well — and I can't find much to admire in him but I care for him as some people like opium or drink although they would like not to. *N'en parlons plus*. Randolph's condition and my precarious future

63

worries me much more . . . My life is dreadful here'.

Temporarily even she collapsed, from neither eating nor sleeping, though a spirited denial appeared in *The Times* that any such weakness had occurred. She was tended by Clara in a small room at the top of the house, while the Churchill family kept company with the Duchess, waiting for the inevitable news.

On 24 January 1895, Lord Randolph died. Jennie and her sons attended the burial service in the village church of Bladon, within sight of Blenheim. Her ten-year-old nephew, Shane Leslie, who was Randolph's godson, was taken to the memorial service held in Westminster Abbey at the same hour, and retained an unforgettable, if romanticised, impression of seeing her later.

She lay in bed in Grosvenor Square: the most beautiful vision of woman I have ever seen: raven black hair caught with diamonds over her face whiter than death, and eyes that shone like wet ebony.

The next day, with Winston and John, she left London for Deepdene, Dorking, the home of Lilian Duchess of Marlborough, widow of the 8th Duke, who was a warmhearted American.

To escape from the suffocating gloom and monastic seclusion imposed by Victorian mourning, Jennie went late in February to Paris for a few months, taking a flat in the Avenue Kléber where she was joined by her sister Leonie and her children. Shane Leslie, the eldest, remembered that on the journey there with his mother they travelled with Paderewski, who had been the idol of the sisters and a protégé of Jennie's when he first visited England.

'. . . grandmamma carped a little at your *apartement* in "the gayest part of the Champs Elysées"' Winston wrote to her, but gaiety was what she needed and meant to have after the bitterness of recent events, though she was temporarily recalled to England by the illness and death of her mother. Her father had died four years earlier.

The restorative power of Paris quickly began to take effect, and the healing process was completed by her meeting with the ebullient American-Irishman, Bourke Cockran, a magnificent orator and *raconteur,* who provided an ideal salve for the wound left by Kinsky and who, as host to her son, was to give Winston a memorable introduction to America and to the art of oratory.

Home-loving Winston begged her to arrange 'some common rendezvous for us' and, returning to London refreshed for the winter season, she settled in a house in Great Cumberland Place and began again to entertain. The Prince of Wales became a frequent guest, evidently appreciating the good food and good gossip she provided, as a change perhaps from the favours he sought from other ladies.

Twice a week two professionals came to practise pianoforte trios with her. She gave her services on various musical occasions and with her friend, Mrs Pearl Craigie (who wrote under the pseudonym of 'John Oliver Hobbes') and Mlle Janotha, once played Bach's Concerto in D for three pianos at the Queen's Hall with an orchestra conducted by Sir Walter Parratt. For exercise she skated at Princes' with a skill acquired in childhood from the versatile Mrs Ronalds. Her hobbies, she told Beatrice Heron Maxwell in an interview for *The Lady's World,* were travelling and collecting jade.

She took trouble with her teenage niece, Clare Frewen, afterwards Clare Sheridan the sculptress, who was born in the eighties after her mother had, in the best Victorian tradition, ridden to hounds that day, and whose home was close to hers. Every morning Clare had to read aloud from *The Times* to her 'beloved, worldly aunt' while she breakfasted, so that the girl should not appear too ignorant of public affairs when dining out. As an exponent of the

Age of Worth, the famous coutourier, Jennie also advised her about dress. Clare, as soon as she got over being intimidated by her was subjugated: 'One had to admire her; she was resplendent'.

More important than any of these diversions was the realisation that her elder son had developed from a difficult youth, as his parents had regarded him, into a young man of dynamic personality and keen ambition, avid for experience and adventure. He had been gazetted to the 4th Queen's Own Hussars shortly after his father's death, and she now devoted her energy and initiative to promoting his career and helping him through her many contacts to go where he wished and see what he wanted to see. They both had fluent pens and when he set off to see a war in Cuba and later to the North-West frontier in India, he contributed vivid reports to English newspapers, educating himself in the craft of letters as he went along. His mother secured him a job as war correspondent for *The Daily Telegraph,* and while he was campaigning with the Malakand Field Force she was arranging the publication of the book he had speedily written about it. Their combined efforts were to get him attached to the 21st Lancers in order to take part in the Sudan Campaign and, as it turned out, in the Battle of Omdurman. Danger was a challenge they both took up with all flags flying, her own courage and staying power were emerging in him. In the eyes of her son 'She was still at forty young, beautiful and fascinating. We worked together on even terms, more like brother and sister than mother and son'.

The young Duchess of Marlborough, arriving in England after her honeymoon in 1896 to meet her husband's family, found a good friend in her fellow American:

Lady Randolph was a beautiful woman with a vital gaiety that made her the life and soul of any party. She was still, in middle age, the mistress of many hearts . . .

Her grey eyes sparkled with the joy of living and when, as was often the case, her anecdotes were risqué, it was in her eyes as well as her words that one could read the implications . . . Her constant friendship and loyalty were to be precious to me.

Jennie had come a long way from the early years of her marriage, when she had deplored the telling of 'roguey-poguey stories', especially in mixed company.

Another American, Lady Curzon, while her husband was Viceroy of India, used a happy phrase when she wrote to her 'You are the only person who lives on the crest of the wave and is always full of vitality and success'.

She was often a visitor at Keele Hall in Staffordshire, rented by the Grand Duke Michael of Russia and his wife Countess Torby. The Baroness de Stoëckl, whose husband was equerry to the Grand Duke, remembered a visit when 'she brought her son — red-haired and rather blunt.   I remember one morning coming into a large drawing-room at Keele and Winston Churchill, quite a young man, was lying on the sofa with his legs over the arm. He simply nodded "Good morning" and never moved from that position. I was shocked beyond words'.

Of his mother the Baroness observed: 'She was a beautiful woman and played the piano divinely. She was witty, alive, and in love with young George West'.

IV 🌺 A Very Pretty Wedding

When her old friend, Frances Warwick, quizzed her about a second marriage Jennie Churchill had declared, 'I am not going to marry anyone. If a perfect darling with at least £40,000 a year wants me very much I might consider it . . .'

Now a perfect darling had come into view, though not, alas, with £40,000 a year, and she had fallen in love with him.

The attraction was mutual. Cornwallis-West confessed that it was flattering to find himself an object of interest to this mature and famous woman, actually a little older than his mother, who talked to him of her ambitions for her son and encouraged him to tell her of his own. Doubtless her attention boosted his self-confidence while her knowledge of the world, in both senses of the phrase, endowed her with an aura of romance. It was delightful too for her to have the company of this young man of superb physique with, like herself, a love of fun when things were going well.

Like any collector of fine specimens Jennie felt she had to have this one; but something very like £40,000 was necessary to her just then, for she had embarked on a highly costly venture, confident that it would bring in rich returns if launched regardless of expense.

Lady Warwick extended a delicate feline claw to point it out. 'It was one of Lady Randolph's amusing foibles to be regarded as literary. It was during her "literary period" that she started a magazine in conjunction with a young

68

man friend . . . that was called *The Anglo-Saxon Review.*'

As is now clear from letters published with the first volume of Randolph Churchill's biography of his father, it was in fact Winston who did all the preliminary work for launching the magazine, interviewing the publisher, John Lane, 'a gentlemanlike fellow', and advising his mother on financial terms. 'I don't think you should allow all the money to be guaranteed by outsiders. It strengthens your position in every way if you could guarantee say £500.' He pauses to deliver a homily:

> If it [goes on] you will have an occupation and an interest in life which will make up for all the silly social amusements you will cease to shine in as time goes on and which will give you in the latter part of your life as fine a position in the world of taste and thought as formerly and now in that of elegance and beauty . . .

'The *Review* took the form of a quarterly miscellany. At the suggestion of Lane, 'a great authority on bindings,' Winston discovered, each volume had a handsome tooled leather binding, a replica of the work of some master of the craft such as Derome or the English Samuel Mearne, with an article by Cyril Davenport, the British Museum expert. Paper and type were of the highest quality.

Distinguished men rallied to its support: Lionel Cust, Director of the National Protrait Gallery, and Arthur Strong, Librarian of the House of Lords and Chatsworth, made themselves responsible for art and historical matters respectively, while John Morley, and Sir James Knowles of *The Nineteenth Century* advised on finance. The highest in the world of affairs were approached for contributions: Lord Salisbury, who was Prime Minister and too busy to comply, Lord Rosebery, who wrote on Sir Robert Peel for the first number but later perceived 'the cloven hoof' of politics in the journal and cancelled his subscription, and Cecil Rhodes, who parried the question.

69

Other contributors were Henry James, Elizabeth Robins, Whitelaw Reid and Pearl Craigie who had encouraged Jennie in the project. Professor (later Sir) Oliver Lodge provided an article on wireless telegraphy and Algernon Swinburne a rather hackneyed poem celebrating the battle of the Nile. Bernard Shaw sent an article on Verdi and a long letter on not accepting invitations to luncheon. Nothing daunted, she did arrange for her son to meet Shaw at luncheon, when in spite of his earlier antipathy he was instantly attracted by the sparkling gaiety of G.B.S.'s conversation.

In introducing the first issue in June 1899 she gave her reasons for launching the *Review* and bluntly quoted Dr Johnson: 'No one but a blockhead ever wrote except for money'. The price was four guineas per annum, payable in advance.

An American notice suggested that no one but the upper ten was to put pen to it, and E.V. Lucas provided some amusing verses in reply:

Have you heard of the wonderful Magazine
Lady Randolph's to edit with help from the Queen?
It's a guinea a number, too little by half,
For the Crowned Heads of Europe are all on the staff;
And everyone writing verse, fiction or views
The best blue-blooded ink must exclusively use;
While (paper so little distinction achieves)
'Twill wholly be printed on strawberry leaves . . .

A copy of the September 1899 issue, containing her bookplate with gilded cherubs and a phrase of music, was autographed 'to G.C-W from J.S.C.' The *Review* continued for another two years by the end of which time it was running at a loss too great to be sustained and its progenitor had other interests.

In May 1899 the Prince of Wales had stayed with the Cornwallis-Wests at Ruthin and great was the local excitement and delight. The Prince was accompanied by Lord Marcus Beresford, who managed his horses, and by Mr Reuben Sassoon, who placed his bets. Lady Randolph Churchill was also in the house party, although George's parents were deeply worried by his infatuation, for now he was ardently in love as hundreds of his letters to her in her family archives testify.

That summer Jennie and George went about constantly together and people began to talk. A gossip-writer gossiped in a women's magazine:

> As a young and attractive widow it has been impossible for Lady Randolph Churchill to escape the talk that inevitably circulates about one so placed, and there is not a little truth in the old adage that 'there's no smoke without fire'. Certainly Lady Randolph is young looking enough to be taken for her son's fiancée. . .

'Toeing the monotonous gilded line that led from Ascot to Goodwood and to Cowes', as Osbert Sitwell put it in *Great Morning,* they all assembled there in force. Mrs Cornwallis-West was a keen yachtswoman and Princess Daisy usually came for the race week. The Prince invited George aboard *Britannia* and pointed out to him the inadvisability of marrying a woman so much older than himself, and begged him to do nothing in a hurry. But while, after dinner on the yacht *Valhalla,* H.R.H. sat contentedly in a rocking-chair on the deck, smoking a cigar and listening to light music, his host, the Marquis 'Boni' de Castellane, was hearing a new development in the story.

> Moved by the enchantment of the hour and her prospective happiness, Lady Randolph Churchill told me of her engagement to a man twenty years younger than herself . . . 'But you must promise not to tell a living soul', concluded Lady Randolph. . . Judge my surprise, however, when I discovered a few hours later that my secret was everybody's secret, Lady Randolph having

told all my guests exactly the same thing.

Winston Churchill had schooled himself to view with a mature tolerance any course of action his mother might take which would make her happy, whatever his private opinion might be. He frequently made allusions or sent messages to George in his letters, obviously to please her; but in this summer of 1899, while assuring her that whatever she did he would support her in every way, he begged her to 'reflect most seriously on all aspects of the question' and especially on 'the business aspect, on which, as you know, I lay paramount stress. Fine sentiments and empty stomachs do not accord'.

The Marlborough relatives had been consulted and supported him. As Winston did not wish to parley with the other side, there was correspondence between himself and Colonel Cornwallis-West about the marriage which the latter and his wife were understandably doing all in their power to prevent. The titanic Churchills apparently looked down on the country gentry of ancient lineage in spite of, or rather because of the fact that they had 'netted' — Winston's word — a duke and a prince for their daughters; but 'it is for George to settle with his family: and you to consult your own happiness' he told his mother. The West parents were distraught at the prospect of the marriage and the unlikelihood of an heir and Winston believed that family pressure would crush George; but with Jennie to encourage him, it could only be seen as an obstacle to be overcome. Hyper-sensitive as Cornwallis-West was, it is obvious from the Churchill correspondence that he was only too keenly aware of his contemporary's attitude to the marriage.

In the autumn of the same year the South African War broke out and, to his rather naive surprise, he received a letter from the Prince of Wales telling him he had had an opportunity of recommending him to Lord Methuen who was to command the First Division and had asked for an aide-de-camp from his old regiment who could ride, and that he envied him going out on active service. No doubt H.R.H. hoped in his wisdom that immediate absence from the country under such promising auspices might put an end to an unsuitable attachment.

Because of all the rumours Cornwallis-West, before going out, was asked for and gave an undertaking to his Colonel that he would not marry or get engaged before he left England. Everybody, in fact, took great pains to save this young man from the situation in which he was involved. He went off to the war and arrived in time to take part in the Division's first engagement, at Belmont, which looked impregnable: 'without a preliminary bombardment of high-explosive shells it seemed a forlorn hope to attempt to take it; but we had no high explosive shells'. The British artillery were then armed with 'the old twelve-pounder'. However, a frontal attack, in which several of his friends were killed, compelled the Boers to retire, after which the victors, contrary to his expectation, rode back to where they had started from and had breakfast.

In the early stages of the advance on Modder River he was detailed to deliver a message to the General and was obliged, on arrival, to let his pony be led away lest it drew fire on the great man. Later he could not find it and after wandering for hours in the sun was put in hospital for ten days with sunstroke. Eventually he found himself returning to the Modder River in a train, the driver of which soon left it and disappeared into the veldt. Here was the chance he had been waiting for since boyhood. The gradient was very steep and the freight train very heavy, and if it did not get to the top it would block the main supply line from the Orange River to the front. Technical difficulties were great: 'there was not a drop of water in the tank and very little showing on the boiler gauge' but his stoker was game, pointing out that they could 'only be blown up once', and they just managed to crawl to the top of the bank. When they arrived they found the town of Modder River strongly occupied by the Boers.

Years later he wrote about his baptism of fire as a young soldier in this last Victorian war. It had its lighter moments, as when his battalion captured two South African millionaires and a wagon-load of delicacies with which, having reluctantly had to join up, they had equipped themselves: but another, very different memory stayed with him. On returning from an engagement with the enemy at Graspan he came upon 'a magnificent specimen of an old Dutchman lying dead, with a look of marvellous calm upon his face, very like Rembrandt's picture of Jacob Trip in the National Gallery. For the first time it struck me that we were fighting against men. . . whose sole idea was to protect their country from invasion. I thought of this man lying there: what did he probably know about the political intrigue at Pretoria? What did he care about the gold mines around Johannesburg? . . . His was certainly a just cause. I found myself wondering whether ours was'. George was beginning to have misgivings.

Lady Randolph, meanwhile, had become chairman of a committee of Anglo-American Wives formed at the instigation of Mrs Sidney Blow with the object of equipping an American hospital ship, the *Maine,* to bring home the wounded. It included among its twenty members two Duchesses of Marlborough, Mrs Joseph Chamberlain, Mrs Ronalds and the other two Jerome sisters, Mrs Moreton Frewen and Mrs John Leslie. A chalk drawing of Jennie by Sargent was made for the programme of a concert organised by Mrs Brown Potter in support of the project. A very large sum of money was raised and Jennie herself accompanied the ship to South Africa. Just before she left came the news that Winston, who was in Africa as war correspondent for *The Morning Post,* had been taken prisoner by the

74

Boers, but almost as quickly, the story of his dramatic escape. 'We know that she was equally anxious to see young George Cornwallis-West' said Consuelo Marlborough about Jennie's voyage, but they did not meet in Africa.

She spent the winter on board, supervising the transport of the wounded, and before she left for England Cornwallis-West had been invalided home with serious illness resulting from his sunstroke. He was sent for to Marlborough House to recount his experiences to the Prince, who was doubtless anxious to find out whether the war as a cure for love had been successful: but 'Look after George. Write to me all he says,' Jennie was admonishing her sister Leonie as the *Maine* tossed on the high seas. She herself returned to England in the spring of 1900.

The Prince of Wales had told Cornwallis-West when trying to dissuade him from a precipitate marriage that if he went to the war there would be plenty of time to consider the matter when he came back. Apparently there was not. 'Jennie and I had discussed it many a time and she always said that the difference in our ages made marriage out of the question, but after nearly a year's separation she changed her mind.' A sidelight is thrown on his ambivalent attitude at this time by a letter received from his father who had opened by mistake a telegram from Leonie Leslie intended for his son, suggesting that he should meet Jennie when the *Maine* docked at Southampton.

'I wish seriously to ask you' the Colonel wrote to Leonie, 'if you consider a marriage which I am told is again talked of between Lady Randolph and my son can possibly lead to the happiness of either? To begin with she is older than his own mother. She will lose the name in which she is best known to the world and its rank and position and she will find herself married to a man of such an impressionable nature that only a few weeks ago he proposed marriage to a young and pretty girl who refused his attentions notwithstanding his protestations of love. . .'

Whatever the state of George's feelings, absence had but made Jennie's heart grow fonder.

That year, Consuelo Manchester, *née* Ysnaga, one of the anglophile daughters of an American senator with Cuban connections, took a house near Windsor for Ascot week, and invited George and Jennie to stay. He was able to ride over to Pirbright for parade and return in time for the afternoon races. The familiar round had begun again, but a well-staged surprise enlivened it.

On the Thursday morning of that week, as he remembered it, just twenty-six years after Jennie Churchill had appeared on another Gold Cup Day in her wedding dress with roses nodding in her bonnet, he read the announcement of his engagement to her in the press.* Years later he used the incident in an unpublished play.

Again the gossip writer gushed, with some truth, that the engagement was one of the sensations of the year. 'He is very near in age to the two sons of Lady Randolph who are both at the front, and he himself was invalided. . .'

The announcement was immediately followed by a summons to see the commanding officer of his battalion, who told him outright that if he married Lady Randolph he would have to leave the regiment.

If, as a result of their separation and the maturing experience of war, he had had any doubts as to the wisdom of what he was about to do, they were blown to the four winds by what he regarded as an unwarrantable piece of interference. He 'dashed off in a hansom' to the War Office to enlist the sympathy of the Adjutant General, Sir Evelyn Wood, in person, an action which unleashed upon him the wrath of Colonel Fludyer, who commanded the

*I have been unable to find the announcement in *The Times, The Daily Telegraph* or *The Morning Post,* though reference was made in fashionable journals to such an announcement.

regiment, when he heard of it.

Jennie, meanwhile, had also been taking action at a high level and received a letter from Lord Lansdowne telling her that he had spoken to the Commander-in-Chief, who was very sympathetic, and advising her to disregard 'vague threats' such as she had mentioned to him. Unfortunately there was nothing vague about the Colonel's reaction. Captain Cornwallis-West had gone over his head to an official whom he strangely referred to, in their interview, as an enemy of the Brigade of Guards, and he made it clear that his presence was no longer desired or expected.

An appeal to the Prince now brought the realistic response. Was it his intention to make soldiering his profession for the rest of his life? If not, why make enemies of men who had been his friends? The Prince advised him to go on half-pay and look around to see if he could find something else to do, this would give him time in which to reach a decision. The advice was taken. Winston, on hearing that he was leaving the army, wrote from Chicago:

> I seize a moment to write to you from this strange place of pigs and tell you how glad I am you have come to this decision. Unless you are absolutely resolved to be Commander in Chief or upon the other hand are quite convinced that 'orderly officer' is the limit of your capacity the army is a miserable waste of time... I am quite sure that you will soon find some suitable occupation . . . giving a better chance to your own talents.

Just before he sailed for home Winston received a telegram from his mother saying that she proposed to marry George at the end of the month. Arriving at Southampton in the *Dunottar Castle* late in July he was met by her and 'Mr Cornwallis-West' and expressed the opinion, for the benefit of waiting reporters, that the Boers would cause a lot of trouble yet. A week later, on 28 July, 1900, Jennie married George at St Paul's church, Knightsbridge.

A fashionable congregation assembled amid annunciation lilies and 'rare white exotics' in the flower-banked church, and a large crowd of spectators outside it, on a sombre, overcast morning necessitating the use of electric light. The Sub-Dean of the Chapels Royal assisted the vicar and the service was fully choral, with familiar hymns and a Handel anthem to be sung while the register was being signed. The United States Ambassador and, of course, the Portuguese Minister and Count Mensdorf were present, and innumerable women friends, including Miss Muriel Wilson whom his family had hoped George would marry.

The Morning Post and *The Daily Telegraph* vied with each other in their detailed description of the scene. The bride wore 'a chiffon gown of a pale blue shade over silk, elbow sleeves of transparent lace . . . skirt finely tucked and inserted with Cluny lace . . . round the hem of a lace flounce and underneath it frills and ruches of blue chiffon'. With it went a toque composed of tucked chiffon, Brussels lace, white roses, a pale blue osprey and a handsome diamond ornament in front. She wore a pearl and diamond necklace and carried a few white roses and a prayer book 'in accordance with the new fashion, although printed copies of the service were placed on their *prieu-dieu* chairs before the Rood Screen'. Jennie never did anything by halves.

She was given away by the Duke of Marlborough. All her adopted clan were there, Marlboroughs, Blandfords, Roxburghes, 'drawn in a solid phalanx' in Winston's phrase, and after the address they sang 'Now thank we all our God'. She left for the honeymoon in an equally fabulous costume (with a handbag full of bills for George to pay) and among her wedding presents was a diamond and pearl tiara from the Duke and Duchess of Devonshire, A.J. Balfour and other friends.

78

'My father and mother had done their utmost to prevent it, which was quite natural on their part, but I well remember my feeling of intense regret at none of my family being present when I married,' was Cornwallis-West's comment in after years. His playing of his part on the day was, of course, impeccable, and Winston reported to his brother Jack, who was in South Africa, that their Mama had had a very pretty wedding and that George looked supremely happy. 'As we already know each other's views on this subject, I need not pursue it.'

V ❧ Business and Pleasure

How to live in the expensive world of fashion to which he now belonged was the problem that faced Cornwallis-West on his return from honeymoon. Characteristically, he and Jennie had announced their intention to spend a year going round the world, but facts had to be faced rather sooner.

Randolph Churchill described Jennie's marriage to 'the handsomest man of his time' as 'improvident and unsuitable' and added that he was, after paying her debts, to be very hard up.

He had begun to raise funds by way of a mortgage on the reversion of his grandmother's estates as soon as he came of age, for his father kept him very short of money, either because he found his wife's needs sufficiently demanding or because, as a conscientious Victorian parent, he believed that satisfying the demands of the young would lead them to perdition. But a young officer's debts to his tailor and horse dealer were insignificant compared with the needs of a wife who had run through the remains of her previous marriage settlement and had negotiated a large loan to repay smaller ones by taking out as security an insurance policy on her son's life as well as her own and requiring him to guarantee both premiums out of his modest assets. After the marriage Winston generously told her that if she would relieve him of this burden he would ask no allowance from her 'until old Papa West decides to give you and G. more to live on'.

Both young men were sympathetic towards her reckless-
ness, such was her charm. Winston wrote to her, 'We both
know what is good and we both like to have it. Arrangements for payment are left to the future. . . I sympathise
with all your extravagances even more than you do with
mine'; and Cornwallis-West, looking back on her as a remarkable woman with many talents had only this to say
of her failing:

> In money matters she was without any sense of propor-
> tion. The value of money meant nothing to her: what
> counted were the things she got for money . . . If some-
> thing of beauty attracted her she just had to have it; it
> never entered her head to stop and think how she was
> going to pay for it. During all the years we lived to-
> gether the only misunderstandings that ever took place
> between us were over money matters. Her extrava-
> gance was her only fault and, with her nature, the most
> understandable and therefore the most forgivable.

Within a year of their marriage he had to resort to money-
lenders and was seldom if ever to know a moment's peace
of mind where money was concerned for the next twenty
years.

André Maurois in his study of the period suggested
some of the reasons for the luxury and lavishness that
characterised Edwardian society. Large fortunes, founded
on industry, commerce or banking, had been built up in a
generation or two by men of modest origins and a third
generation was now anxious to enjoy the fruits. Moreover, the discovery of the South African gold and diamond
mines enriched both speculators and, indirectly, the whole
nation. The King approved the social rise of financiers who
had taken his fancy, among whom were Baron Hirsch and
Sir Ernest Cassel.

Deprived of the career for which he had been trained,
and adrift in this society, Cornwallis-West acquired a

touching belief that if he could penetrate the mysterious world of finance he too might make money on a scale which would enable his wife to spend as lavishly as she had been accustomed to. At dinner one night he had an opportunity of discussing his prospects with Cassel, who expressed the opinion that most young men with his background should never go east of Temple Bar, a sentiment echoed by millionaire McEwan, father of Mrs Ronnie Greville, to whom he also confided his ambition.

On hearing that he was interested in engineering, Cassel gave him an introduction to the Managing Director of the British Thompson-Houston Company, suggesting that he should get some technical experience; as a result he found himself working in overalls on the construction of the Glasgow Corporation Power Station. This he believed was Cassel's way of testing whether or not his intentions to take up a business career were serious. Under Cassel's aegis he met George Herring, one of the original promoters of the British Electric Traction Company, formed for the creation of tramways in the British Isles, and was offered a seat on the board of the company operating in the Potteries towns, at a nominal remuneration. He demanded not only a seat on board meetings but an office in the Stoke-on-Trent building where he could learn the job. When his car broke down one morning, finding that he would be late for work, he did 'the only possible thing' and with military conscientiousness chartered a special train, which cost him a quarter of his year's fees.

Other directorships came his way and within four years he was earning a reasonably good income, but it was capital that he wanted and needed. Inevitably he presented a sitting target to the adventurer who, with equal inevitability, turned up.

Instead of consulting Cassel or any other of the city men he now knew, perhaps because he guessed what they would

82

say, he determined to give up salary and go after capital and allowed himself to be persuaded, with his susceptibility to blarney not necessarily Irish, to join forces with a born gambler, a clever glib north-countryman named Wheater. He had come to London from the north, hoping to start 'a sort of minor issuing house', and saw in Cornwallis-West a gullible young man who, moving in high society, had the entrée to many city offices where he could claim the attention of men such as Lord Rothschild. Even more to the point, he was able, and apparently willing, to obtain a further mortgage of £35,000 on his reversion, with which to finance the venture. Thus the firm of Wheater, Cornwallis-West & Co. was founded. Lord 'Natty' Rothschild was their first customer. In their first year they made over £23,000, a fact which he afterwards regarded as a disaster.

If the profits were considerable, so were the demands of the partners, and as time went on they embarked on various expensive side-lines which they believed would bring in the desired fortune more quickly. There was, for instance, the copper-mine in Spain, among 'hills covered in spring with sweet-smelling gumcistus'; excellent if there had been more copper in it: the culture of black baroque pearls off the north-east coast of Australia — but the owner of the secret died unexpectedly without divulging it; and the patenting and manufacture of the West-Ashton automatic gas-operated rifle, which was refused by the Small Arms Committee on the grounds that an automatic rifle would encourage the waste of ammunition by the soldier (this was only seven years before the First World War). In fact, in later years when emotion was recollected in tranquillity, Cornwallis-West naively devoted a whole chapter of his memoirs to 'Unsuccessful Enterprises'.

Meanwhile there was 'good news to hear and fine things to be seen' and George and Jennie with their mutual zest for life settled down to enjoy them, though that phrase is quite out of character where two such spirited beings were concerned. 'She had a host of friends, and thus', he said, 'I became an Edwardian, a member of that particular set in society with which the King associated himself' though in his case the King was a family friend.

There were as always plenty of amusing ways of losing money and Jennie and George neglected few of them. Racing and betting, whether at Newmarket, Paris or Buenos Ayres was a must; gambling at cards a habit, organising mammoth money-losing entertainments, for Jennie, great fun, and backing bizarre ventures, for George, a chimerical short cut to riches. 'Be happy with that Darling of a George' Leonie wrote to her sister, and undoubtedly she was.

The last of the family weddings had followed not long after their own, when in February 1901 Shelagh Cornwallis-West married the young 2nd Duke of Westminster who, as a neighbour at Eaton Hall, Chester, had played with her in childhood. Indeed, Daisy tells how, robed in a tablecloth, she once staged a schoolroom wedding for them, with much dressing up of bride and bridesmaids and, with the butler and a stray housemaid as witnesses, solemnly conducted them through the marriage service, using a borrowed ring to unite them. At their real wedding in St Margaret's, Westminster, the pages wore suits copies from Gainsborough's 'Blue Boy' which then hung on the walls of Grosvenor House; Victoria Sackville West, the poetess and novelist and a cousin of the bride, was one of the bridesmaids. The enormous wedding cake modelled the ancestral homes of both bride and bridegroom, a profusion of diamond necklaces figured in the list of marvellous wedding presents, and Bend Or* gave his bride, in her

*So nicknamed from his grandfather, the 1st Duke of Westminster's horse, which won the Derby in 1880, the year after his birth.

sister's view, jewels fit for an empress.

Queen Marie, of Roumania, a granddaughter of Queen Victoria, left a striking picture of the Duchess and her sister at the first big ball given by the Westminsters at Grosvenor House, their London home:

In this ballroom, with its beautiful pictures looking down upon us . . . the very cream of London society had flocked together, including some of the most beautiful women in the world.

Foremost among these was Princess Daisy of Pless, tall and magnificently English in her pink and white bloom. Gold-clad, with a high diamond tiara on her honey-coloured hair, gay, smiling, kindly disposed to all men, she was indeed . . . an incarnation of those days of peace, wealth and general prosperity.

Our hostess, Daisy's sister, was her dark counterpart, she also a tall and brilliantly effective woman . . . One of the sights which has remained in my mind was the exquisite supper-hall erected for the occasion . . . at a table the two sisters, Daisy and Sheila, the fair and the dark, all eyes turning towards them, they fitted so entirely into the beautiful setting . . . The enormous blue and silver flower-filled room was a feast to the eye, complete harmony such as only the most perfect English taste and tradition could achieve . . . There is a sort of peace in perfect attainment, particularly when one has known struggle and the uncomfortable shabbiness of things not yet well established; this faultless achievement of beauty for me was *peace*.

There was an ironic rightness in Queen Marie's reverence for peace, for it eluded her throughout much of her turbulent life.

The Marchioness Curzon, herself a beauty painted by Sargent, Lavery, Laszlo, and by Bennett, a fashionable Edwardian painter, also remembered this magnificent ball, 'with the Duchess looking wonderful, and her sister a dream of beauty,' and felt she would 'never see such grace, dignity and perfect carriage again'.

She had visited Colonel and Mrs Cornwallis-West at Newlands, following a stay with the Norths at Wroxton Abbey. 'This house could not have been a greater contrast in every way' she wrote of Newlands. 'We were so gay there, we seemed to laugh all day long, and this was entirely due to the wonderful high spirits of our hostess, a witty and amusing Irishwoman'.

In the parlour of the Hand Hotel at Chirk I found in the bookshelf, where some bygone guest had left it a lifetime ago, a bound copy of *The Lady's World,* the equivalent of today's fashionable 'glossies', illustrated with pictures of ladies standing like pouter pigeons in voluminous frilled blouses with long pouches over skirts tightly gored on the hips and cascading around their unseen feet, and enormous upturned hats, like inverted meatplates, bearing bows, fruit, flowers, feathers and lace.

The pages opened at the portrait of 'a particularly important baby girl', Lady Ursula Grosvenor, the first child of Shelagh and Bend Or.

This little lady has a pair of especially beautiful grandmothers, the Countess Grosvenor and Mrs Cornwallis-West. At present she is the only tenant of the great nurseries at Eaton Hall but it is naturally hoped that in due time an heir will be born to the Duchess of Westminster.

In due time an heir was born to the Westminsters and King Edward stood sponsor for him, but he was only to be lost to them by a sudden illness five years later. Their last child was a girl.

*In 1886-7 there had been an attempt to reconstruct it as a serious magazine under the editorship of Oscar Wilde, who changed the title to *The Woman's World,* but it did not pay, and reverted to the original title.

With the accession of Edward VII to the throne, the younger set as well as the King's contemporaries could look forward to an era energetic in the pursuit of pleasure, luxury and novelty. The marriage of several Americans, and also of several members of the Gaiety Theatre company, into the peerage was infusing new blood and new outlooks. There were three American Duchesses of Marlborough within a space of forty years. The Duchess of Roxburghe, two succeeding Duchesses of Manchester, the Marchioness Curzon and the Countess of Essex were some of the many titled Americans; while from the stage came Lady Churston later Duchess of Leinster (Denise Orme, *née* Jessie Smither), the Countess of Dudley (Gertie Millar) and the Marchioness of Headfort (Rose Boote).

Motoring was now the fashion. Cornwallis-West had been given his first motor car ride in 1898, by the 1st Baron Montagu of Beaulieu, a pioneer of motoring. In 1900 he bought a single-cylinder de Dion car and spent three weeks in the repair shops of a Paris garage to master its eccentricities. Thereafter cars were an added incentive to him and his wife to join the weekend boom and visit their friends and relations.

They went frequently to Blenheim where the Marlboroughs, Sunny, 9th Duke, and Consuelo, entertained lavishly and the wit of Jennie's elder son and his friend F.E. Smith (Lord Birkenhead to be) scintillated. 'Winston', his hostess remembered, 'was then the life and soul of the young and brilliant circle that gathered round him at Blenheim: a circle in which the women matched their beauty against the intellectural attractions of the men'.

At Cliveden, bought by the Astors from the Westminsters, Winston was percipiently observed by Princess Daisy:

I am awfully sorry for him: he is like a racehorse wanting to start at once — even on the wrong track; he has so

87

much impetuousness that he cannot hold himself back, and he is too clever and has too much personal magnetism . . . he may someday be Prime Minister — and why not, he has the energy and the brains.

In the oppressive magnificence of Keele, they were frequently entertained in company with the King and Queen. Bridge was the order of the day and Cornwallis-West remembered travelling back from a house-party there on a hot Sunday afternoon in the royal train, passing slowly through the larger stations so that people could see the King, who was playing bridge and had to put his cards hastily out of sight at each halt.

On one occasion they were bidden to Sandringham to a party to celebrate the King's birthday and Jennie reported to Winston that there had been 'nice weather — pleasant people and excellent sport. George shot very well & [we] are both in good favour — so that is all right'.

When Shelagh was at home, the Wild West Show were often reunited at her huge house parties at Eaton Hall, but she was seldom for long in one place. Wilfrid Scawen Blunt, writing from Clouds, home of the George Wyndhams, in his prodigious *Diaries* draws a hectic picture of a day in life of a duchess:

George arrived in the afternoon from Elbarrow. With him Shelagh, Duchess of Westminster. They had been at the manoeuvres all the morning and then had motored over here . . . stopped for tea and were to motor back and go out to dinner . . . She had with her in camp a lady's maid, a footman, a chauffeur and a cook. The Duke, in the meanwhile, is away motoring in Ireland with another chauffeur, another cook and more servants, besides a motorboat . . . The life of both of them is a perpetual gallop.

Theatricals were a favourite form of entertainment and they reached a high standard, the amateurs competing with the professionals who were invited to join them. At Eaton Shelagh acted 'beautifully' with Norman Forbes in Dion Clayton Calthrop's *Scaramouche,* and George and Daisy appeared in Alfred Sutro's *Open Door.* At Chatsworth, in a party that often included the King and Queen, it was also customary to produce contemporary plays, one of which was by Lady Bell, mother of Gertrude Bell, the explorer. King Edward, after watching a play in which Jennie and Mrs Willie James had taken part, wrote to his 'darling Daisy', Lady Warwick, that everybody there seemed mad about acting. It was, however, H.M. reflected, a welcome change from the gambling.

At Gopsall, with the Howes, charades were played, and news of them found its way into an American magazine, where the following widely quoted and occasionally denied paragraph appeared. I repeat it for the characteristically flamboyant picture it draws of Jennie:

> Historically, the success of the evening was Mrs George Cornwallis-West, formerly Lady Randolph Churchill, who came as a roystering Spanish cavalier. She wore black silk tights, doublet and hose, a dark crimson cloak . . . had a sword, a great diamond blazing in her black sombrero with its drooping feathers; diamond buckles in her pretty shoes, and a black moustache, waxed and ferociously curled . . .

Wit was highly regarded in Edwardian conversation, and Cornwallis-West treasured an example of brilliantly apt retort heard by himself and Jennie when they were staying with the Tweedmouths at Guisachan in Scotland (Lady Tweedmouth was one of Jennie's sisters-in-law). Lord Rosebery was a guest, as was a youth of about seventeen who had arrived at the acne age. After dinner Rosebery uttered 'some marvellous epigram', and the youth at once suggested that he had seen him studying Marcus Aurelius before dinner. 'Rosebery looked at him with those curious cod-fish blue eyes of his and said: "All my life I've loved a womanly woman and admired a manly man, but I never could stand a boily boy". ' This story was later credited to Winston Churchill when dealing with hecklers at election addresses.

Cornwallis-West delighted in the informal house parties held at the end of the season at country houses where there was a private cricket ground in the park. The parties lasted a week, and the relaxed atmosphere, the long hours of out-door activity, the good talk and laughter at the end of the day, provided a setting in which he was at his happiest. When cricket was over, the trout-fishermen would rush to the river for the evening rise until dinner, after which there would be dancing.

At Frampton Court, the Dorset home of the Sheridans, where open house was kept for the neighbours each day of the match, he met and enjoyed the company of Thomas Hardy.

Jennie, who did not share her young husband's passion for the simple life, viewed these gatherings with a slightly sardonic eye:

Innumerable are the country house parties with golf, lawn-tennis and the river to amuse and keep one out of doors. Mothers with broods of marriageable daughters find this kind of entertainment a better market to take them to than the heated atmosphere of the ballroom, which the desirable *partis* shun for the greater attraction of air and exercise.

There was always Sunday to be got through after morning church, and history does not relate whether truant was ever played during the hours the fish were rising. It was out of the question to be seen fishing on Sunday, certainly north of the Border, and Loelia Duchess of Westminster has a touching little story of her notoriously autocratic husband in Scotland. 'Once it was so perfect that it was almost more then Benny could bear and I saw him take his smallest salmon rod to pieces, hide it under his coat like a guilty schoolboy, and walk nonchalantly down to a hidden pool.' That was in the nineteen-thirties.

Autumn brought the joys of the moors. Shooting had begun for Cornwallis-West when a guest at Ruthin allowed him to fire off his gun, which killed the pheasant but knocked out the ten-year-old. A few years later he was given a gun of his own and, tutored by the Ruthin head keeper, became as years went on a first class shot. After his marriage he had plenty of opportunities for sport on the finest estates and, if he was confined to London by business, shooting was still available within sixteen miles of Marble Arch.

Whenever in later life he took up his pen to describe some incident in sport, the country sights and sounds come sharply to life. 'On a bright day in October, with the leaves turning, stubble still a pale yellow and the turnip fields brilliantly green, the surroundings are truly fascinating. . . When [a partridge] comes over a fence and sees the guns his sharp cry seems to say "Good God! What's that?" and he alters his flight, and that is where the skill of the shooter comes in. (I speak of course of English partridges; a French partridge never alters his flight and is very easy to hit.)'

VI ❧ Edwardian Hey-Day

After living for a time in London Jennie and George made their home in the country where they could do some week-end entertaining themselves.

Salisbury Hall, the house they found, was a collector's piece, a small moated manor a few miles south of St Albans.

It was recorded in the Domesday book as already existing in the time of Edward the Confessor. A Tudor mansion was built on the site by Sir John Cutte, under-treasurer to Henry VII, and in the seventeenth century Jeremiah Snow, a goldsmith-banker who bought it from the banker Hoare, called in Nicholas Hawksmoor to advise on its reconstruction. Snow entertained Charles II there, and Nell Gwynne's son, the first Duke of St Albans, was said to have been born there. Cornwallis-West was convinced that he saw her ghost, with a blue fichu round her shoulders, watching him as he descended the staircase one evening at dusk.

In their Visitors' Book, a parchment-paged volume in a handsome gilt-tooled leather binding with brocade endpapers, the owners wrote the name of their home, the date, 16 July 1904, and their own names. The first visitors to sign it were Jennie's sisters, followed by Prince Arthur of Connaught and a party of young Leslies and Churchills, including her sons John S. and Winston S. Churchill, the latter signature with five little lines beneath it.

From then on, signatures in bold, individual hands spring alive on the page, not eschewing underlinings and flourishes: Warrenders and Harcourts, Lennoxes and Lyttons, Manchesters and Roxburghes, Lady Sarah Wilson, born a Churchill, Mrs Hwfa Williams, a hostess of renown, the West sisters and their husbands — Daisy draws her name flower — Ethel Barrymore, whose devoted admirer Winston Churchill was, and Edward Marsh, his small scholarly handwriting contrasting with the larger flowing scripts, accompanying Winston to whom he was to act as secretary for many years.

Marsh left his own description of Salisbury Hall, the 'perfect little manor house' and 'delicious garden', and also of his hostess, for whom he conceived a lasting affection:

She was an incredible and most delightful compound of flagrant worldliness and eternal childhood, in thrall to fashion and luxury (life didn't begin for her on a basis of less than forty pairs of shoes) yet never sacrificing one human quality of warm-heartedness, humour, loyalty, sincerity or steadfast and pugnacious courage. By the time I knew her, the first volume of her beauty was closed, but years afterwards she opened a second. . .

The Marquis de Soveral, the Portuguese Minister, and Count Albert Mensdorff, the Austrian Ambassador, appear inevitably, for no party was complete without them, and especially de Soveral, the attractively ugly 'Blue Monkey'. In the Duke of Portland's opinion 'He had a real genius for society . . . being a most pleasant and charming companion he kept all the ladies happy, and young and old, they rejoiced in his company . . . a more loyal friend could not be found'.

An important 'Curzon' occupies the middle of a page (he had been Viceroy of India since 1898). Two childish signatures painfully carved with a thick nib, 'Blandford' and 'Ivor Churchill', represent the future 10th Duke of Marlborough and his brother. A single page contains the signature of the King and the date 'May 27th 1906', and the party on that occasion included Mrs Alice Keppel, the Willie Jameses, Consuelo Marlborough, Prince Francis of Teck, Mensdorff, and Sidney Grenville. Once, in 1903, the highly individual signature of Lily Kinsky, the name by which the Count's wife, Elizabeth, was known appears, and at the foot of the page is his rather ill-formed 'C. Kinsky'.

Two distinguished foreign actresses were also among their visitors, Jeanne Granier, who signed the book, and the famous Eleanora Duse, who was not in a condition to sign anything. It was at the time of her parting with the poet, D'Annunzio, and she was a very unhappy woman. She arrived in tears and remained secluded in the drawing-room, visited at intervals by the ladies of the party. None of the men, not even her host, was permitted to see her. It was not Jennie's first experience of the great actress's temperament, as a similarly frustrating scene had occured at Aix-les-Bains when she had arranged a meeting between Duse and the King of Greece, but she generously summed up on that occasion, 'Genius excuses everything'.

Interspersing the signatures are snapshots of young women with pyramids of hair and skirts brushing the lawn, ladies in enormous hats reclining in punts, young men in stiff white collars leaning on garden seats or sitting, capped and goggled, in high motor cars. The moat looks beautifully clear and a beau punts Clare Frewen on it. She comes frequently, and in December 1904 Wilfred Sheridan, her future husband, is a guest, with her mother. Dogs are ubiquitous. Bess, the hosts' Labrador, poses with her noble head held high, or is snapped looking speculatively at the ducks on the pond, or politely facing away from the camera so that Susie, a Scottie, or Charlie the dachs-hund, can have the limelight.

In a wintry scene General Scobell, a tall man, faces the camera in what was probably an astrakhan-collared coat

94

reaching to his ankles, and beside him stands Lady M. Orr Ewing, equally tall and imposing in velvet and furs. The picture of an elegant snow-woman made by feminist Jennie for Christmas 1906 occupies a page to itself.

Time slips by and Gwendeline Bertie and Clementine Hozier make their appearance. Lady Gwendeline arrives with her mama in June 1907 and presumably Jack Churchill is at home. Clementine and Winston sign for the first time in February 1908. In May Clementine comes again and Winston's signature takes a fantastic turn, presumably a 'knocked silly' wobble; in June her brother William is a guest. Soon Gwendeline's name is followed by Jack's and the drawing of a heart pierced by a dart, symbol of their engagement. Winston and Clementine draw secret signs after their names and in August her mother, Lady Blanche Hozier, visits frequently. Wedding bells are about to ring for her daughter, and on 25 October 1908, back from honeymoon, Clementine Churchill, 'sweet almond-eyed gazelle' as the young musician, Denis Browne, was to call her, signs her new name with a flourish. As we know from her husband the decision had been taken to live happily ever after.

When he came to write his memoirs Cornwallis-West included a chapter on 'Things Spooky and Practical Jokes', and things spooky were now very much in vogue. As early as 1881 the planchette board had been in use at Welbeck to amuse the Prince. The Duke of Portland described it simply as a game, which some guests played while others played whist or listened to the singing of Mrs Ronalds. In the new century, planchette and table turning became, for a time, the rage, and Cornwallis-West remembered the young Duchess of Marlborough obligingly turning the tables to spell out the name of an Ascot winner. Horoscopes were cast, hands read and soothsayers and the

95

crystal ball consulted. Oscar Wilde took such consultations sufficiently seriously to write to Edward Heron Allen, who had published *A Manual of Cheirosophy*, asking him to cast his first child's horoscope: '. . . it was born at a quarter to eleven last Friday morning. My wife is very anxious to know its fate and has begged me to ask you to search the stars'.

A few years later the young Winston Churchill spent two guineas out of his meagre resources on a palm reading and was evidently impressed by the 'strange skill' of the palmist, Mrs Robinson, but could not bring himself to agree to have his 'hand published to the world', presumably in the book she was later to produce.

The *Palmist's Review,* which had appeared during the year 1899-1901, had included diagrams of the palms of well-known people as diverse as Émile Zola, Rubinstein the pianist, and President Kruger, and in an earlier version of it, the *Palmist and Cheirological Review* of 1895, those of Mrs Langtry, Mr Gladstone and George Bernard Shaw, the latter's accompanied by a most interesting — in the light of his future development — sketch of his character and potentialities. It ended:

> The fate line is all in pieces in both hands; the subject makes his own career in the world and tries to carry out to some extent the eccentric ideas that are created by the peculiarities of Luna and the Head line, to some extent because, in a hand of Apollo, there is always a great deal of pose for effect as well as what is genuine. The Fame line . . . is growing and doubling, the subject should do some very good artistic work . . . if he will leave the practical side of things to others and stick to art as he should . . . There is no foretelling, by the help of character in hands like these, what a subject may do . . . and the Fate line being absolutely unformed, he has his career entirely in his own hands to make or mar, accord-

1. George's great-great-grandfather, the 2nd Earl De La Warr

2. George's parents, Col William and Mrs Patsy Cornwallis-West

3. Ruthin Castle, in North Wales, the Cornwallis-West family seat

4. Captain John Whitby, R.N. and his wife, Mary Anne Theresa

5. Newlands Manor, in Hampshire, Admiral Cornwallis's bequest

6. George's literary grandmother
Mrs Frederick Cornwallis-West   7. The Prince of Wales, 1899

8. George, aged fifteen, with his mother and sisters, 1890

9. George's elder sister, Daisy, and her husband, the Prince of Pless

10. George's younger sister, Shelagh, and her future husband, the 2nd Duke of Westminster

11. Young Lady Randolph Churchill

12. Jennie (Lady Randolph), ready for the theatre

13. Jennie's true love, Count Charles Kinsky

14. Lord Randolph Churchill, aged 43, two years before he died

15. Jennie as the Empress Theodora on the evening she first observed George, in 1897

16. George and Jennie during a royal visit to Ruthin Castle in May 1899. *Left to right:* Hon. F. Guest, Col. W. Cornwallis-West, the Prince of Wales, Mrs. W. Cornwallis-West, Lord Marcus Beresford, Miss Muriel Wilson, Shelagh Cornwallis-West, Jennie, George

MARLBOROUGH HOUSE.

17. The Prince of Wales's letter to George before he was sent to S. Africa in 1899

18. George on Toby, the pony awarded eleven clasps in the Boer War, 1899

19. Winston Churchill, the unsuccessful candidate for Oldham, 1899

20. George and Jennie at the time of their engagement, 1900

21. George in the Scots Guards, after the Boer War

22. George's stepson, the successful candidate for Oldham, 1901

23. The Countess of Warwick (King Edward's 'darling Daisy') as Semiramis at Mrs Adair's fancy dress ball

24. Mrs Lillie Langtry, on stage

25. George and Jennie's country home, Salisbury Hall, Herts

26. Stella (Mrs Patrick Campbell), the Second Mrs Tanqueray, as George saw her at the age of 18

27. George Bernard Shaw in the 1890s

28. Stella on the eve of her marriage to George, 1914

29. George in the 1930s

30. George Bernard Shaw

31. The gamekeeper at Ruthin   32. George in the 1940s.

[Handwritten letter specimen]

33. Specimen of George's handwriting, from a letter to the author

John 2nd Earl De La Warr m. (1756) Mary Wynyard
b. 1729

Hon. Frederick West m. (2rdly, 1798) Maria Myddleton
b. 1767

Frederick Richard West m. (2ndly, 1827) Theresa John Cornwallis Whitby
b. 1799

William Cornwallis West m. (1872) Mary FitzPatrick
b. 1835

Rev. Frederick FitzPatrick m. Lady Olivia Taylour, dau. of 2nd Marquess of Headfort

Mary Theresa Olivia (Daisy) m. Pr.nce Hans Heinrich of Pless

George m. (1stly, 1900) Jennie Jerome m. (1stly, 1874) Lord Randolph Churchill
b. 1874

Constance Edwina (Shelagh) m. 2nd Duke of Westminster

(2ndly, 1914) Mrs Beatrice Stella Patrick Campbell
(3rdly, 1940) Mrs Georgette Hirsch

Winston Leonard Spencer Churchill   John Strange Spencer Churchill

ing, not as circumstances treat him, but as he chooses to treat the circumstances of his own life.

Shaw was then thirty-nine. In another three years, he had begun the tidying-up of his fate line by committing himself to the care of Charlotte Payne-Townshend to look after 'the practical side of things' and by publishing his seven *Plays Pleasant and Unpleasant.*

Practical jokes, to modern minds one of the more painful features of life in Victorian and Edwardian times, were popular both among princes and Pooters. In the inventive West family they were sometimes of a high order, but Queen Alexandra liked those of a cruder kind. In particular she was said to enjoy the informal parties to which the de Greys invited her, when some hilarious joke, such as the dropping of a load of specially provided china by a well-coached footman, was staged for her benefit. Being deaf, poor lady, she perhaps savoured this dramatic crash more than her hosts' *recherché* musical entertainment.

Lady de Grey, born a Herbert of Pembroke and widow of the 4th Earl of Lonsdale, had married as her second husband, Lord de Grey, later the Marquess of Ripon, and Coombe House, their home on Wimbledon Common, was for nearly thirty years a meeting place for music lovers of taste and fashion. Oscar Wilde called her and Lillie Langtry 'my two Beauties' and it was to her that he dedicated his play, *A Woman of No Importance.* There is a passage, redolent of Proust and Monet, mentioning her in a letter of his to Bosie (Lord Alfred Douglas) in 1894. 'I lunched with Gladys de Grey, Reggie and Alec Yorke there. They want me to go to Paris with them on Thursday: they say one wears flannels and straw hats and dines in the Bois.'

She was an old friend of Jennie's, and Jennie and George were among the regular visitors to her Sunday musical parties. Here Melba and Caruso, and the brothers Jean and Edouard de Reszke would sing, and Reynaldo Hahn would bring his own orchestra to play his own compositions; here Kreisler played his violin, to the swooning appreciation of his wife, as George remembered, and W.S. Gilbert delighted with his singing of old French ballads. In later years, Irene Scharrer and Gervase Elwes continued the tradition and played and sang at Coombe.

Music was not the only art that Gladys de Grey encouraged. When in 1899 César Ritz had opened his magnificent Carlton Hotel restaurant, with Escoffier as chef (it was some years later that Vietnam's Ho Chi Minh, then a wandering scholar, worked in the kitchens under him) Gladys de Grey supported it by taking for one evening the Lyric Theatre, with the whole cast and orchestra of Messager's opera, *Véronique*, which had just appeared in Paris, inviting her friends to it and afterwards to supper at the new restaurant. Thereafter people seen in the Palm Court included the Prince of Wales, the Duke of Cambridge, Sir Basil Zaharoff, the mysterious international financier, the King of Spain, the Emperor of Ethiopia and Prince Henry of Pless; and among the ladies who entertained there were Sarah Bernhardt, Melba and Jennie Churchill.

Although the London Ritz (for the building of which American engineers were imported to employ the new method of all-steel construction) was not opened until 1905, the turn of the century had perhaps been the crowning point of the genius of Monsieur Ritz. All over Europe his superbly built and staffed hotels had opened within the last ten years and he had attracted to his service a unique architect, Mewès, chef, Escoffier, and head waiter, Olivier of the Paris Ritz. In her fascinating biography of her husband, his widow, Madame Ritz, offered an interesting theory:

Escoffier and Ritz were simply products of their time . . .
I was made to realise this by a few sentences in a little brochure, *Dissertation sur l'Art Culinaire*, which fell into

98

my hands not long ago . . . sent me by the author, Eugène Herbodeau, who is not only the chef at the Carlton Hotel, but a man of cultivation and one of Escoffier's most loyal pupils. In it I read: 'Etudiez bien la marche de la civilisation, et vous verrez ses progrès liés à ceux de l'art culinaire'. And he goes on to show how the times create the men they need in the realm of cookery and hotel-keeping. According to Herbodeau, the art of that time, the literature . . . the clothes, the furniture, all were affected by a sudden yearning for realism and simplicity. Zola, Daudet, Goncourt, Cézanne, Monet, Manet, Degas, Whistler — each in his separate and different ways was striving for these things. Dress reform was being practised, if only by a few. And the Japanese influence was not only felt in Whistler's art, but in interior decoration . . . the idea at the back of it was a sincere desire for lightness and simplicity. Just at the same period people were beginning to revolt against the heavy, long, elaborate meals that were the rule and to desire something lighter, more simple . . .

After being shown by M. Herbodeau his collection of Escoffier menus — he discussed them 'as if they had been symphonies' — ordered and signed by many of the most famous people of the day, she ordered for herself that night at the Carlton 'among other things, *rossolnick clair, canard à l'Orange,* and, of course, *pêche Melba'.*

Escoffier, too, fittingly produced a *Guide Culinaire* which was a masterpiece of simple and direct expression as well as of culinary art. Its dishes combine a diary with a Debrett: *'Mousseline de volaille Patti . . . poularde Tosca . . . Filets de sole Véronique . . . Selle d'agneau Edward VII . . . Coeurs d'artichauts grand-duc'.*

Many such nostalgic delicacies could be added to the list, *Suprêmes de volaille Jeannette, Soufflé Rothschild, Gateau*

99

Bibesco, but I will quote only, from the English edition of the Guide, a menu for 'a Fancy Supper', to be taken, perhaps, *tête à tête* with a dazzling beauty escorted from the stage door of the Gaiety Theatre, in her cartwheel hat and black silk stockings, to whom, with the Zeltinger Schlossberg 1897 or the Bollinger Extra Dry 1898, might be offered heart and coronet — or a diamond necklace.

Caviar Sterlet

Crêpes Muscovite

Consommé aux Pommes d'Amour

Sylphides à la crème d'Ecrévisses

Mignonette de poulet Petit-Duc

Cailles dodues escortées d'Ortolans

Nymphes rose — Désirs de Mascotte

Pointes d'Asperges à l'huile Vièrge

Charmes de Vénus voilés à l'Orientale

Plaisirs des Dames

Etoiles Filantes — Frivolités

VINS

This aphrodisian repast may yet stir a memory, for its prototype was served at the Carlton Hotel on Saturday 6 October 1906.

Eating habits in English private houses were not, however, immediately influenced by the new trends towards simplicity. Cornwallis-West recalled that guests arriving at Halton, Afred de Rothschild's 'palace', moved from a wonderful tea to a Lucullan dinner, including, in July, a dish named *Poussins Haltonais,* which consisted of young pheasants which had had their necks wrung, 'quite illegal to kill, but excellent to eat'. They were entertained by a private orchestra and sometimes a circus, with their host as ringmaster, in costume, benignly cracking a whip. They had only to mention to him any deficiency, such as the absence of a private golf course, to find on their next visit that it had been remedied.

100

Dining at Tring Park with Lord Rothschild, the first professing Jew to be made a peer, Cornwallis-West found himself seated on his host's right hand and was puzzled until he discovered the reason. Rothschild himself dined only on milk and biscuits, and as one delicious course succeeded another he savoured it vicariously, by getting his junior guest to describe its succulence. Obviously he could not very well ask Lord Revelstoke or Sir Ernest Cassel to act as taster.

Another Rothschild brother, Ferdinand, was established at Waddesdon, in Bucks, and nursed the illusion, as Lady Walburga Paget tartly observed, that his house was the finest modern thing in England. 'He is effete, like his brother; they cannot eat, sleep or do anything simply, like other mortals. They will hardly survive another generation.' The other side of the coin was that this highly cultured man, who was a Member of Parliament and a trustee of the British Museum, assembled at his home a superb collection of ancient jewels, plate and other works of art which he bequeathed to the nation on his death.

Nothing conveys better the character of these gatherings than Sir Harold Nicolson's description of the routine of the weekend party in a rich country house, 'and all houses in the Edwardian epoch were rich'.

Tea was served in the blue gallery. Then there would be bridge, and later dinner, including among its innumerable dishes ptarmigan, which appeared at every meal, beginning with breakfast. Then more bridge, and at midnight: there would be devilled chicken, and more sandwiches, and every form of spirit and mineral water which man or woman could desire. In the corridors upstairs the ladies-maids would hang listlessly yawning. Fires would sparkle in the grates, reflected in brass bedstead and mirror. The pink silk reading lamps were lit beside the beds. Upon the night-table stood bottles of Malvern

Water and of Vichy, covered dishes of sandwiches. A ribboned coverlet of swansdown would be draped across the sofa. The kettle by the fire purred.

Next morning the valets would pack their Eno's and their shooting sticks . . . Their carriages would meet them, horses champing bits, at the arrival platform at Paddington . . . And next Saturday it would all begin again.

Mrs Lynn Linton, the prolific woman journalist of the day, writing in *The Sketch,* expressed the view that 'In these days, when all the world has become crazy for "Bridge" there is something soothing in an old-fashioned game of whist'.

In spite of all the gaiety in these early nineteen-hundreds Cornwallis-West's health was often in a bad way. Before going to Eton he had been operated on by the local doctor in an armchair in the study of Newlands, without an anaesthetic, for the removal of his tonsils. In the middle of the operation the wound bled so profusely that the doctor took fright and left the second tonsil alone, with, he believed, disastrous results. He suffered throughout his life with throat infections and with sinus trouble which, as is often the nature of that complaint, varied in proportion to the amount of worry or stress that afflicted him; and this generally depended on the state of the battle between income and expenditure.

In 1906 Bend Or, although at the time there was a coolness between them, unexpectedly came to his brother-in-law's aid in a roundabout way on hearing of the latest financial disaster that had befallen him. Almost predictably, a solicitor to whom Cornwallis-West had entrusted several thousands of pounds for the settlement of some debts, absconded, and from Bulawayo in August the Duke wrote to Winston that he 'wanted to help in some small way the difficulties that have fallen to George West in losing £8,000. I hear you and your brother Jack have between you come to his rescue . . . I send you the enclosed cheque to be used on condition that George should never know of this transaction till I choose, if ever, to let him know'.

In the correspondence that ensued Winston's habitual caution prevailed. On 18 October he sent George a cheque for £3,000 towards paying off the sums of which he had been robbed. 'The transaction is personal between us . . . a loan to be repaid at any time at three months' notice on my request. Meanwhile you should pay me interest at 2½% . . .'

To Bend Or he reported sending the money 'at 2½% and out of it he has repaid me the smaller sum with which I have been able to assist him. . .' He added the hope that the day would come when he might be allowed to tell George who had helped him and so 'remove all clouds between two honest-hearted men. Happily the rift was repaired before Christmas on the Duke's initiative.

The following year was a particularly bad one for Cornwallis-West. Jennie told Winston that he had not drawn a penny from his business. It was during this time that he was obliged to have a nasal operation.

In the spring Jennie would go, with or without her husband, who preferred fishing in Ireland, to the Riviera, 'gambling and wearing lovely clothes', as Princess Daisy reported. The casino at Monte Carlo, where she liked to play, had been in existence since 1861. Queen Victoria's preference for the neighbourhood further west had started the popularity of Cannes, but in spite of the development of the Corniche routes that town had excluded a casino until 1906. King Edward, though a faithful supporter of Cannes, often went to Biarritz in March and April, to the annoyance of the Riviera hotel keepers as there was a general exodus to the Basque coast in his wake. The difference as Cornwallis-West saw it was that if a stranger went to Cannes everyone tried to find out how rich he was; if he went to Biarritz, the point at issue was whether or not he was a good fellow.

At her villa in Beaulieu in 1907 Daisy commented in her Diary: 'Jennie, my sister-in-law, who married George and still loves him immensely, poor dear . . . is uncommonly nice and still very handsome, but of course the difference in age is a sad and terrible drawback . . .'

She had paid a visit to her old home which her father had decided to close up.

Poor old Ruthin, the home of his ancestors for centuries, with its moat and dungeons and lovely flower gardens . . . now it seems as if the spirit of disaster hangs over it. In the old rooms where we played 'house' and had tea-parties I looked about me and thought sadly that the little feet of my nephews and nieces would never patter on those boards.

Although she had her own three sons by her German husband they could not quite make up for the lack of direct heirs to her adored parents.

In a fit of homesickness while in Seville the following spring she remarked that even George, 'with whom everything is not quite as he would wish it,' had his little home near London; but the little home was beginning to cramp its ebullient owners and the expenses of entertaining had proved surprisingly heavy. In a fit of economy they planned to let Salisbury Hall and live at the Ritz. In fact they were about to leave it for ever. Winston and Clementine signed the visitors' book for the last time on 27 November 1908.

The autumn of 1908 saw the publication of *The Reminiscences of Lady Randolph Churchill,* by Mrs George Cornwallis-West, dedicated to her two sons.

During her life she had surveyed the national and

104

international scenes from exceptionally fine vantage points, and her husband had encouraged her to write the story of it, spanning, as it did, the political and social events of nearly sixty years; though probably little encouragement was needed. Unlike the memoirs of some of her contemporaries, hers contained no indiscreet revelations, though a fund of them must have been stored in her memory.

Characteristically her preface began:

In studying the Prefaces to various contemporary Memoirs, I find that most of them are apologetic in tone and I ask myself — why? If a book needs an apology — ought it to be written?

Having been favoured by Providence with delightful and absorbing experiences, having travelled all over the world and met many of the most distinguished people of my generation, why should I not recall all that I can about them, and about the stirring things I have seen, or shared in doing?

That is what she did, and her recollections were, to use the *Morning Post* reviewer's meticulous phraseology, 'instinct of the *joie de vivre* and there is not a dull page in them'.

The book was well received and widely reviewed in the newspapers and journals. Today it is of even greater interest as a piece of social history, both domestic and European, than when it first appeared.

That winter they took the Asquiths' house in Cavendish Square and, encouraged by the success of her book, Jennie wrote a play and determined to see it staged. Seeking, naturally, the highest talent for the venture, her choice fell on the celebrated Mrs Patrick Campbell, whom she already knew, for according to Seymour Leslie in *The Jerome Connexion* Mrs Campbell 'with a horrid Peke' was one of the distinguished visitors who might frequently be found sitting on the sofa — 'they called it a *canapé* because

French words sounded more elegant' — at the 'sacred six o'clock' of one or another Edwardian lady.

Anita Leslie in her biography of Jennie quoted a mysterious reference, from a letter written by her sister Clara in the early nineteen-hundreds, to 'George's little flirt with Mrs Pat Campbell' but apparently Jennie never heard of it or did not take it seriously. She read her play to Mrs Campbell who, 'feeling it would be a friendly act' offered, according to her own story, to produce it for her and to play the lead. Jennie's husband urged her to accept. The offer proved to be an unfortunate one.

'Mrs Campbell,' Cornwallis-West wrote, 'became a constant visitor to the house. Besides being a very beautiful woman she was a brilliant conversationist and had a keen sense of humour and a ready wit'.

VII ❧ On with the New

On the west side of the square a white house with bright window boxes was the home of Mrs Patrick Campbell . . . She would descend upon Young Street with a swish of silk and a froth and fluff of lace demanding nursery tea, or suddenly require a bed in a darkened room as it was impossible for her to rest in her own house . . .

Going to her house was always an adventure because you never knew who was there or what might happen. Auntie Stella might receive me in bed with curtains drawn, lamentably moaning that she was an old woman and would never be nice to look at again. Or she might be trailing about the house in a long-tailed lace wrapper alternatively scolding and caressing whoever came within reach, lavishing affection on Pinky Ponky Poo, her adored dog, companion for many years. One might find Yeats upstairs and Mr Henri Bernstein downstairs, while, neglecting them both, Auntie Stella might insist on taking me for a drive and reciting *Mélisande* in French — she was going to act with Sarah Bernhardt — begging her most incompetent critic to criticise her French accent.

Such was Angela Thirkell's early impression of one of the most spectacular and capricious figures of her time.

'I do love to talk to her,' wrote Max Beerbohm's sister, Constance, 'for she has a devil . . . as long as a person is nice-looking and clever, a devil is a great advantage'.

Up to a point Stella found it so.

Beatrice Stella Campbell, *née* Tanner, was according to

her own story, one of six children born to a Welsh father and an Italian mother, the father being 'the heir of one of the richest Anglo-Indians', the mother 'the daughter of an Italian political exile'.

My Italian mother and her beautiful sisters were invested for me with great romantic glamour . . . My life appeared to have sprung from a magical past, in which Italy, Persia, India — white houses with flat roofs, white-robed Arabs and lovely Arab horses — were all seen through a mist of childish imaginings.

She painted an exotic picture of the lives of her Italian forebears and her six maternal aunts, and this strong sense of drama from her earliest years, combined with the more practical qualities inherited from her father, who was the son of an army contractor to the British East India Company and an early believer in the Darwinian theory, was to mould her into the dominating, brilliant, emotional yet hard cored character whose personality, perhaps even as much as her talent, mesmerised Victorian and Edwardian theatregoers as well as those who met her in private life.

She was born in February 1865 and as a child led a nomadic existence, heavily sentimentalised in her description of it. When she was sixteen she returned home after spending a year in Paris with an aunt, to find her father 'definitely ruined' and her 'dear Uncle Harry's fortune' melted away. A relative paid for her to be trained at the Guildhall School of Music, where she won a scholarship which would have given her three years' free tuition in Leipzig, but it was never taken up because she had already met her future husband, Patrick Campbell. They eloped (almost all the characters in her story eloped) within four months of their first meeting, and were married in Bishopsgate Street.

There is sympathetic sketch of this engaging man in Desmond MacCarthy's *Portraits*. For him, good luck was always just around the corner, and he spent years away from his adored family looking for it in Australia, Africa, everywhere, 'but had he stumbled on the richest valley in Eldorado he would have returned home with nothing in his pockets'.

With the birth of her second child she realised that she would have to help herself and that within herself was the strength she needed. She joined a drama club and received a wonderful notice in *The Stage* after her first performance. Within a year she had obtained an introduction to an agent, making an entrance into his office which would have killed most women's chances stone dead — in floods of tears — and was soon signing contracts. In 1890 she joined Ben Greet's touring company, and from then on her career was assured. In 1893 she was chosen by Sir Arthur Pinero to play the lead in his new play, *The Second Mrs Tanqueray*. Lady Violet Greville remembered:

> When Mrs Campbell swept across the stage in her brilliant beauty and her scarlet drapery, her magnificent eyes flashing, her voice full of passion and meaning, an unspeakable thrill stirred the audience, it was like a breath from another world . . . new, revivifying, inspiring. When the curtain came down after the first act there was silence and then thunderous applause.

Among the audience, taken by an enlightened father to see this daring play, was the eighteen-year-old George West. 'We're getting on, dear boy!' said his parent as they came out, 'I wonder what they'll give us next.' But the boy had been given more than enough. He heard the play discussed at every luncheon and dinner table and lively arguments took place as to whether it should have been passed by the censor, but everyone praised the superb presentation of Mrs Campbell's Paula Tanqueray.

Meanwhile, through the success of the play, she had made the acquaintance of several people in high society, where the stage was beginning to be accepted as a respectable profession. 'She was well aware that the playgoing public came to see her rather than the play,' wrote Janet Dunbar in *Mrs G.B.S.* 'She was ambitious to be received into society and missed no opportunity to gain the friendship of prominent people'. Among them were Lord Pembroke, Lord Wemyss and the Burne-Joneses. Linda Waterfield, author of *Castle in Italy,* remembered her being taken by Lord Wemyss to visit G.F. Watts, the artist whom she was anxious should paint her as Lady Macbeth. 'She used all her charm and threw herself at Signor's feet, telling him how wonderful he was. The dramatic effect was lost as he was very deaf. He bent towards her saying "What, what, my dear?" '

In April 1900 the flow of eagerly awaited, loving letters and cables that had punctuated the years with unfulfilled promises ceased. Patrick Campbell was killed in the Boer war: but by then she was established as London's leading actress.

In her reminiscences Mrs Campbell dealt condescendingly with Jennie's play, which she produced in July 1909.

> An exaggerated importance grew around the production owing to Royalty and many distinguished people being interested in it . . . Jennie, I fancy, imagined producing her play would be of some social advantage to us all: I was intolerant of what I thought was nonsense and showed it quickly.

If Jennie was included in that 'us', this fancy was an absurd one since she, accustomed to high society in Paris from an early age, in addition to having married into a ducal family and frequented royal circles, had no more social worlds to conquer. Stella, on the other hand, according to her daughter-in-law, 'dearly loved a title and her titled friends loved her'. (She would be wonderful value

110

at a dinner party.) Feeling herself borne up on the crest of the Edwardian wave, she was unlikely to have been entirely unconscious of the fact that her connexion with the play might yet add socially to the lustre she had achieved professionally.

The play, a comedy in three acts, entitled *His Borrowed Plumes,* appeared at the Hicks Theatre (now the Globe) in Shaftesbury Avenue, with a cast of fifteen, which included Henry Ainley, Sara Algood and Mrs Campbell's daughter, Stella Beech, as well as, of course, herself. Society flocked to see a play written by one brilliant woman and produced and acted in by another; but in Cornwallis-West's opinion it was kept on too long and became an unsuccessful enterprise.

After quoting from a diverting criticism of it by Mr Walkley of *The Times*, Stella's narrative continued:

Then, in the unexpected way things sometimes happen in this world, George Cornwallis-West was seriously attracted by me. I believed his life was unhappy and warmly gave him my friendship and affection. This caused gossip and pain, that cannot be gone into here.

Except for Daisy's cautious hints in her Diary, all concerned are naturally silent on the relations between Cornwallis-West and his wife at this time, but in the nature of things such a marriage was likely to come to grief sooner or later, and the burden of Jennie's extravagance, and his own inability to cope with it, strained this to the limit.

How then did it come about that he fell a second time into the arms of a predatory matriarch, usually, like himself, up to the eyes in debt?

Stella confided in him, appealing perhaps to his chivalry and his vanity. Confidences invite an exchange and it must have been all too easy to confess his own frustrations, whatever they might be, to her receptive ear. As a Welsh Irishman he could not help being a born actor, and here

111

was a magnificent leading lady with whom to play the classic scene of the disenchanted husband. He could not but slip into the part in spite of himself and find it turning into real life.

Then there was the attraction of her circle of friends whose interests were mainly artistic. At Stella's charming old house in Kensington Square he met many famous actors and writers, among them James Barrie and Bernard Shaw, and succumbed at once to Shaw's wit and kindness.

The liking was mutual. They shared the Irish sense of the ridiculous, could speak with the same brogue and enjoy the same jokes. Shaw, aware of Cornwallis-West's vulnerability, was at pains to avoid hurting or discouraging him. From now on he was to attempt the delicate balancing feat of acting not only as dramatic critic and literary adviser but as guide, philosopher and friend to both the protagonists in their ill-starred association.

In 1909 Cornwallis-West saw the Derby won by King Edward with a horse called Minoru. The enthusiasm of the crowd was tremendous, especially when the king himself led his horse into the paddock. It was the third and last time he was to do so.

A great many pens have sketched the figure of Edward VII, both as *bonhomme* and *grand seigneur.* Daisy Pless treasured a last memory of him at her sister's at Eaton Hall in December 1909. He asked her how she was spending the afternoon, and when she told him she was going to visit her aged Grandmother FitzPatrick, who was living in a cottage a few miles away, he insisted on going too, staying to tea and listening to the old lady's reminiscences of her girlhood at the court of Queen Victoria when her father was Lord Chamberlain. The Princess liked to remember how successfully he made Lady Olivia feel that

112

even if youth had fled, her charm remained.

To little Sonia Keppel he was 'Kingy' who enjoyed incognito picnics by the side of a main road packed with carriages and early motor cars with, of course, such necessities as chairs and tables, footmen and silver plate, and who brought exciting presents when he called on her mama. To his friend Christopher Sykes, of Brantingham Thorpe, who squandered his fortune and submitted to having brandy poured over his head to entertain him when Prince of Wales, he was an object of love and veneration. The king could do no wrong.

Having been deprived of authority for nearly sixty years of his existence, while acquiring a stifling amount of culture and, as an antidote, a considerable experience of life and an interest in people, he enjoyed his brief reign and took its responsibilities very seriously.

He loved opera and the magnificence of Covent Garden when the house was ablaze with the colour of uniforms, dresses, jewels and flowers. On the evening of 27 April 1910, a few hours after returning from a visit to Biarritz, he went to Covent Garden to hear Tetrazzini singing Gilda in *Rigoletto*. Lord Redesdale, in a privately printed memoir on the king, recalled seeing him in his usual corner seat in the omnibus box, 'looking very tired and worn. He sat through one act all alone. Then . . . he opened the door of the box, lingered for a little while with a very sad expression on his face . . . took a last look at the house as if to bid it farewell, and then went out'. Ten days later Edward VII died.

George Cornwallis-West mourned the best friend of his youth. Jennie, living ever in the present, set about welcoming the new régime by promoting a huge ball in the week of the next king's coronation, with the object of raising money for a Shakespeare Memorial Theatre fund. Already in 1909 the Hon. Mrs Alfred Lyttelton had

113

circularised Shaw and other stage personalities suggesting that 'an association should be formed called "The National Shakespeare Theatre Association" of those ready to pay £1 a year'. (As I write, a national theatre is at last taking concrete form on the South Bank of the Thames.) The ball was held at the Albert Hall on 20 June 1911 and was attended by King George V and Queen Mary and their royal guests, and by some four thousand others. The participants represented famous Tudor characters or grouped themselves according to Shakespeare's plays, George and Jennie joining the *Twelfth Night* party as Sebastian and Olivia. The late Lord Mersey, to whose lot it fell to escort two Malay Sultans to the ball, found they enjoyed it 'only moderately, regarding it as a rather inferior theatrical performance', but a week later Jennie was able to announce through *The Times* that a net profit of £10,000 had been made for the cause.

Delighted, no doubt, with her success, she followed it up in 1912 with the most ambitious of all her enterprises, the Shakespeare's England Exhibition and Tourney, staged at Earl's Court in aid of a national theatre. Sir Edwin Lutyens designed the Tudor setting, with the Globe Theatre, the Mermaid Tavern, run as a club, and old cottages in contemporary gardens; and on 11 July a number of noblemen of approved lineage, clad in meticulously correct armour and riding superb mounts, jousted in the Tourney. The West family trio all participated, Shelagh in the Ballet des Chevaux, Daisy leading the Parade of the Princess Errant, and George in the train of Baron Ashby St Ledgers. The Tourney was won by the Duke of Marlborough, though *The Annual Register* contained a curious version of the result:

July 11 at Earl's Court . . . a tournament was held in which the Duke of Marlborough was beaten by Mr F.G. Guest, who, unknown to the audience, had taken the place of his brother, Lord Ashby St Ledgers. The prize, a gold cup, was ultimately adjudged to the Duke.

The *Register* also noted, on 12 July, that the temperature in London rose to 88° in the shade; the fine weather, however, did not, as the Exhibition did, last until October. The general public did not go to it, and everyone concerned, including the bankers, Cox & Co., who, according to her husband had been beguiled by Jennie into backing the venture to the tune of £35,000, lost their money.

Feeling the need to get away from it all, Cornwallis-West went abroad at intervals during these two years. He joined a tarpon-fishing expedition in Tampico, went on to New Mexico and thence to New York, returning the following year to shoot wapiti in Wyoming. Back in New York again, he underwent a serious gall-bladder operation at the Mount Sinai hospital, followed by convalescence at the luxurious home of Mrs W.K. Vanderbilt at Long Island.

Stella, to escape the gossip, had also been back and forth to America. She had originally refused the lead in Robert Hichen's play, *Bella Donna,* but on her return to England in 1911 Sir George Alexander had sent it to her again. One Sunday she and Cornwallis-West motored to Burnham Beeches and read it together. He prophesied she would make it one of the successes of her career, but she reproached him for suggesting she should play such a horrible part: 'people might think I am like that', she complained. Nevertheless she decided to accept it. The play opened at the St James's Theatre at the end of the year, and, according to her own admission, made a small fortune.

One night during its run she was involved in a taxi accident which, though not at first appearing to have serious results, led to a mysterious illness during which, for six months, she lay allegedly at death's door.

Mrs Alfred Lyttelton, her devoted friend, wrote of it to Shaw:

I wish she would get well now but she won't just yet . . . She has been ill through and through, body, mind and spirit — a regular cataclysm it has been — and severe just in proportion to the strength and vigour and richness of her temperament.

On her attitude to money Mrs Lyttelton continued:

As you know by now she is not merely extravagant but a terribly glad giver. She has kept and still keeps all sorts of obscure retainers and relations and she simply has not saved because she has given and given and given.

She was still ill in December 1912 when, 'one day George came to see me . . . I had not seen him for a very long time; he seemed deeply moved and unhappy. His words, "Live, Stella, live and help me," touched me to the roots of my being'.

I can hear her opposite player speaking his lines from the depth of his tender heart, unable to bear the spectacle of this magnificent creature lying pale and ethereal among the lacey pillows, hypnotically taking his cue from her faint protest that she had no wish to live ('and there would be all those bills for this illness to be faced'); but about this time an old correspondence had taken on a new lease of life and another Irishman was writing:

I never encourage illness. When I saw you last you you were in bed, but you had the energy of ten tigresses; and your remarkably fine neck would have carried the pediment of the Parthenon like a feather if you had been snatched up from between the sheets and set up as a caryatid. It is I who need sympathy . . . Get up and console ME.

Ever, G.B.S.

Cornwallis-West in his memoirs was naturally silent about the five-year interval between his acquaintance with and

116

his marriage to Mrs Patrick Campbell, but in the famous battle of words that raged between her and Shaw his name is often mentioned. When Shaw's professed passion for her was at its height (could it have been the stimulus he thought she needed to give of her best in his new play?) he begged her not to talk of marrying George. 'No sooner do you mention George than I see with a frightful lucidity all the worldly reasons why you should marry him . . . Though I like George . . . I say he is young and I am old, so let him wait . . .'

Stella, however, had no intention of doing any such thing. She fled in alarm from Shaw's compromising pursuit of her to Sandwich in August 1913, for Jennie had filed a petition for divorce and the case had been heard on 15 July. Inevitably the newspapers had a field day describing the appearance in court of this 'mother of a Cabinet Minister' with 'eyes still sparkling with fire, lips . . . full of character . . . commanding bearing' as one of them put it. The suit was not defended. Two days later George left England with Princess Daisy, bound for Buenos Aires and a semi-regal progress through South America.

On the granting of her petition an announcement appeared in the Court Circular to the effect that Mrs George Cornwallis-West would in future be known as Lady Randolph Churchill. The following April she changed her name by deed poll. Jennie was alone again after thirteen years of shared fun and affection, whatever the ups and downs may have been. It was popularly supposed that the real reason for ending the marriage was that Cornwallis-West wished to marry a younger woman and to found a family and even she, refusing to recognise what was happening under her eyes, believed it; but the woman he was now committed to marry was forty-nine and his father must have had to resign himself to the fact that there was no likelihood of an heir to the Wests and Whitbys. After

117

knowing Stella for several years, George faced his second marriage with no illusions; once again he had loved in haste and had leisure to repent it, but the affair had gone on too long and it would have taken more courage than he possessed to withdraw from it.

Stella and George were married on 6 April 1914 at the Kensington Register Office, within hours of the decree nisi having been made absolute, for the reason that, as she explained, *Pygmalion* was to be produced a few days later and there would then be little chance of a quiet time together. After a brawl with newspaper photographers they drove to Crowborough, stopping, according to one report, for a shrimp tea on the way.

'We were happy at last,' she declared, 'I with my belief in the love I had struggled against for so long — convinced that George had been a very unhappy man.'

Her reasons for entering upon what must obviously have been an insecure marriage from the point of view of both money and age remain unclear. She might understandably be flattered by the admiration of an attractive man more than ten years her junior, she may have found irresistible the piquancy of acquiring the husband of another famous woman, or she may simply, as she would have us believe, have allowed herself to fall in love, though the perspicacious Shaw saw worldly reasons as the draw.

Whatever the basic reasons for George's unhappiness, it was not in Stella's nature to cure them.

VIII ❧ 'Pygmalion' and After

Shaw had written *Pygmalion* with Mrs Patrick Campbell in mind as 'an East-end dona in an apron and three orange and red ostrich feathers'. When he read it to Sir George Alexander at the St James's Theatre the latter was delighted and offered to get Shaw any actress he named for the part, provided it was not Mrs Pat. After his tribulations with the production of *Bella Donna* he felt he'd 'rather die' than endure her tantrums again.

Needless to say, Shaw got his way, and the play opened at His Majesty's Theatre on 11 April 1914, with Sir Herbert Tree playing Higgins to Stella's Eliza, and made theatrical history.

Everybody was there, although it was a Saturday night. On the following Monday morning *The Times* critic devoted a column and a half to the conscientious telling of the story of the play, and deplored the famous epithet: 'O greatly daring Mr Shaw . . . there is a whole range of forbidden words in the English language, a little more of your courage and we suppose they may be heard too'. In the last paragraph he gave seven words to the leading lady, 'Mrs Campbell's Eliza is a delicious thing'. That was all: but it was enough. Her success in the part of Eliza was assured by the paeons of praise that sounded on all sides.

The Daily Telegraph also expressed pain at the use of a 'sanguinary epithet redolent of unredeemed guttersnipery. This, we take it, is Realism in Excelsis!' it exclaimed, but Cornwallis-West observed that everyone present seemed to be expressing delight at finding an author who was willing to shock them, 'and how they enjoyed the process of being shocked!' Shaw had unwittingly paved the way for today's acceptance of four-letter words on the stage.

Soon after their marriage Stella wrote to G.B.S.: 'George is more precious to me than my bones and we are bound together by a deep and gentle understanding of each other'.

No doubt she believed what she wrote; no doubt both were on their best behaviour; but she demanded exclusive attention. When he wanted to read in the train, his book was thrown out of the window; when, as a light sleeper, he wanted a bed to himself, his bedclothes were hurled over the banisters. He used this incident in one of his plays. After a few months they took a holiday alone on the west coast of Ireland with, as she told Shaw, 'dogs, fishing rods, servants, books and plays,' and in the same play he depicted his leading lady's agonies of boredom in a country house setting after the first rapture had worn off.

Within four months, peace and order and pleasant living were to be shattered permanently by the outbreak of the First World War.

To Cornwallis-West it came as no surprise, as he had learned something of the realities of the European situation during his visits to Pless.

'You can't have two top dogs in one kennel' his brother-in-law, Pless, had said when they were discussing the position of Great Britain and Germany *vis-à-vis* the rest of the world. But when the assassination of the Archduke Ferdinand at Sarajevo on 28 June presaged war, the lure of a Hampshire trout stream was too strong for him to tear himself away and return to his business. On the other hand, so sure was he of the sequel that he had a khaki uniform made for himself in readiness.

His partner, Wheater, had not shared his pessimistic view, and the efforts he made to justify his opinion when war actually come, were 'of a very expensive nature and were the direct cause of the ultimate failure of Wheater, Cornwallis-West & Co.'

He immediately rejoined the reserve battalion of his regiment and volunteered in a training capacity for the Royal Naval Division which Winston Churchill, now First Lord of the Admiralty, had inaugurated. It had as its nucleus a force of naval volunteer reservists, many of whom had never actually belonged to the Royal Navy and were unlikely at present, for lack of ships, to be called upon to serve at sea. It was decided to form an infantry division comprising two brigades of these volunteers and a third brigade of Royal Marine reservists. The War Office agreed to co-operate in their training and the First Lord was anxious to obtain the services of ex-Guards officers for the purpose, so Cornwallis-West was given command of the Anson battalion encamped in Lord Northbourne's park at Betteshanger. Rupert Brooke and Denis Browne were among those who joined the battalion, Brooke having been offered a commission by Churchill.

Arrangements were made for the transfer of *Pygmalion* and its leading lady to New York, where the play was to open in October, and Cornwallis-West obtained leave to see his wife off. Bernard Shaw was also at the station, having sent him a particularly fine specimen of a letter, typed on one of his funny green sheets, as Stella called them, the previous day:

10 Adelphi Terrace, W.C.
2nd October 1914.

My dear Cornwallis-West,

Since you expect to go out soon, I really refuse to leave

you troubled in spirit by that man with his eyes gouged out. I have been on his track for quite a long time now. A chauffeur who came to Torquay actually saw him; but on that occasion his wife did not go mad: she exclaimed 'I know now there is no God'. He was in the City of London hospital until one of the governors went to see him there. But he had escaped, and the staff denied all knowledge of him. He is hiding with the baby who had its fingers cut off by the Uhlans. Both are believed to be with the Russian Army we shipped to Belgium through Scotland from Archangel.

Ponsonby, just back with a wound, denies that there are any atrocities, and sets up an opposition story of the remarkable kindness of a German officer to a Tommy whose elbow was smashed.

I have spoken with Miss Boyle O'Reilly, who was present at the sack of Louvain but returned intacta. She saw the nurses whose fingers and hands had been cut off. They had grown new ones and were in prime condition. One had her wrist burnt. She had fooled with a spirit lamp of explosive construction. Miss O'Reilly also interviewed the outraged women. They had all heard of outrages in the next villages to theirs, but had not actually witnessed them, and were, personally, virgins.

The atrocities committed by our troops fill the Berlin papers with copy and the Berlin soul with patriotic fury. We kill the wounded; we poison the wells; we toss babies on the point of our bayonets; we burn field hospitals full of German wounded; we chop off Belgian babies' heads in their mothers' arms. Having previously put on the helmets of slain Uhlans, we make collections of breasts and eyes; we never venture into battle without driving crowds of women before us; we mock the Kaiser's grief for the death of his thirty-seventh and last of his six sons; our men shoot their officers (who persuade them that they are fighting the Russians instead of the universally popular Germans) and surrender with tears of joy to their kind captors; and the Tsar's mother is Sir Edward Grey's mistress.

As you know, the truth about war is always bad enough; but there really isn't a solitary scrap of evidence that the Germans, apart from their obsolete usage of hostage shooting, are behaving worse than we should behave in the same circumstances.

Stella will think that I write this for the sake of arguing. I do so because war is horrible when one does not respect one's enemies, and there is no reason why you should be depressed and disgusted by expecting more than the regulation horrors which are all in the day's work. I hope the very worst that will happen to you will be capture by Pless and imprisonment in his best bedroom until the war is over. But probably you will come back a Lieutenant-General.

Yours ever,

G.B.S.

In the same week, Shaw's Open Letter to the President of the United States on the futility of war, with constructive opinions on peace, was published in *The Nation* under the title 'Common Sense about the War' and was widely misunderstood at the time.

The next day Cornwallis-West set out for the war by special train as his embarkation orders had arrived too late for him to catch the ordinary boat train. This piece of patriotic extravagance was unnecessary, as it turned out, as after passing through Ashford he observed the boat train standing on a side line to allow his to pass, to the obvious annoyance of several 'brass hats' who were peering out of the windows wondering why they had been held up.

When he saw the Division at Dover he realised how sadly lacking the men were in all necessary equipment; no khaki, no slings to their rifles, no packs, mess-tins, water-bottles, or ammunition pouches, though a few of the deficiencies were made up on disembarkation. Churchill himself was in Antwerp on the crucial night of 6 October and wrote of it in *The World Crisis, 1911 - 1914:*

> All through the night the fighting was continual . . . At the Belgian Headquarters I was told that the Belgian night attack had miscarried, that the Germans were attacking strongly, that the Belgian troops were very tired . . . The Naval Brigades had arrived and . . . were now marching to their assigned positions in the line. But where was the line? It was one thing to put these partially trained and ill-equipped troops into a trench line, and quite another to involve them in the manoeuvres of a moving action.

The story of the Antwerp expedition occupied a chapter in Cornwallis-West's memoirs and he concluded:

> At the time, I and many others who had taken part in this business, while proud of the way the men had behaved in such circumstances, were incensed at having been sent on active service with entirely untrained troops.

> In fairness, however, to Winston Churchill it must be said that the sending of the Naval Division to Antwerp may have altered the whole course of the war. I discussed the affair with the late Sir John Cowans, who thought likewise, saying that those ten precious days gave Sir John French sufficient time to move the British Army on to the coast of Flanders and thus stay the advance on the Channel ports. The Germans, who always acted by rule of thumb and with very little imagination, refused to take the chance of leaving a hostile city . . . on their right flank; therefore it had to be reduced . . . The

two brigades of the Naval Division could easily have been accommodated in comparatively few trains, but numbers of trains of incalculable length — entirely empty — streamed over the bridge into Antwerp before the siege actually began, and for all the enemy knew, there might have been twenty thousand troops in the city. It was a game of poker. Winston held the worst hand, but he won by sheer bluff.

Cornwallis-West was among those who escaped internment in Holland, the fate of the 1st Brigade for the duration of the war, and soon Shaw was writing to Stella in America:

> George called here when he got back from that hell; but I was in Torquay and missed him. Then the poor man wrote . . . begging me to let him see the New York notices as you had not sent him any . . . What a brute you are!

G.B.S. had put them in the wastepaper basket, but he managed to satisfy George's request.

Spy mania was rampant in England, and Cornwallis-West suffered excessively from it. The fact of Daisy's son being in the German Army, and the indiscretion of her mother in visiting German prisoners in England, added ready fuel to the fires of suspicion which smoulder during all wars.

> To be congratulated on having got out of a nasty mess like Antwerp was all right, but to be congratulated half a dozen times a day . . . on having escaped execution in the Tower by a firing squad became monotonous . . . It was said that my father had a hidden store of rifles in the cellars at Newlands, which had been deposited when the German Emperor was at Highcliff and had come over for the day to visit my parents. These rifles were supposed to be for the use of German waiters still living in England . . . who were miraculously to mobilise themselves at Newlands when the great day of the Ger-

man invasion arrived.   However improbable it may sound now, it was very real at the time.

Daisy was suffering similarly in Germany, where, although she was nursing German wounded, she was suspected of English sympathies, which she could not help but have, and of anti-German activities which, had the suspicious known it, consisted in nothing more subversive than writing indiscreet and imploring letters to the Kaiser to abate his wrath and allow her to visit her parents in England. The Kaiser, incidentally, on the outbreak of war, had moved into Pless Castle where he had often been a guest. At home, Shelagh Westminster had organised a hospital for wounded officers and her mother wrote to Daisy:

> George's wife Stella made five hundred pounds for the hospital by one matinée in America . . . do you know. I *like* that woman; she is nice to me, which the other one never was, and she worships George and, poor old boy, he is so different and loves soldiering again.

Surely she had read Jennie's flattering reference to her, but perhaps like turned to like? Both Patsy and Stella were creatures of impulse, and his mother was unlikely to perceive that it was the life of action and the escape it afforded from turbulent domesticity that was proving a tonic to her son.

After a winter in camp in England he was seriously ill with bronchitis, and at a medical board was given six months' leave of absence. The spy stories had spread to America, and it was suggested that he should spend the time in that country furthering British propaganda, an assignment he welcomed. He joined his wife, who was now playing in Boston, and she reported to Shaw:

> George looks after me splendidly and the company and the business side — George is an angel — he is a most beloved man — I don't see how I can let him go back to that crazy, vulgar, accursed war.

In Boston he was invited to speak as the guest of honour at the Tavern Club, where an alleged Dutchman gave a garbled version of the Antwerp expedition. He was unfortunate in having in his audience possibly the only man in America who had commanded a battalion in that expedition.

In Philadelphia, at the Fish Club, he had the delicate task of making a speech in celebration of Washington's birthday anniversary, introducing, of course, some propaganda for the Allies. In Salt Lake City he was able to extract an apology from a paper which had cast aspersions on his family, and in San Francisco he received an invitation from President Theodore Roosevelt to visit him at his hotel, where he listened to the President's forceful views about the urgent need for America to come into the war.

Stella was touring America from east to west, and he now turned to good account the family talent for acting. Coached by her, he joined the company and played prominent parts. From St Louis she wrote to Shaw:

George . . . played 'Orreyed' in *Tanqueray* and 'Doolittle' splendidly, much better than Kent . . . and he played the lead in *Search Lights*. Then he got very ill; he worked too hard . . . Now he is playing again. He is so clever . . . and is adored by everyone.

Shaw replied that the exploits of 'George Frederick', the stage name he used, had created some sensation among his admirers at home; but Stella's jealousy would not permit him to share the headlines for long, and he was packed off to continue his convalescence elsewhere.

Eventually he was fit to return to duty in England, leaving Stella in America to complete her tour. From Newlands his mother wrote to her:

Your beloved has just arrived in his uniform, so good to look at . . . his men I hear simply *worship* him . . . Stella dear, you cabled me to spend £30 on George's

127

hut. But it has not come yet. I only tell you because it may be lost in the post.

These ladies rivalled each other in their eccentricities over money matters. Stella presumably wished to give George a garden hut in which to relax when he was on leave.

In April 1916 she came home in order to play in Sir George Alexander's revival of *Bella Donna*. She arrived on the day her husband's bankruptcy was published.

When in 1905 he had chosen to leave industry for finance, the prospects had seemed alluring. The large profits his firm at first made had bred a fatal optimism. One was apt, as he said, to work by the rule of three and to reckon that if it was possible to make twenty thousand in one year, obviously in three years it would be sixty thousand, 'and then the thought arises as to how many years it will be necessary to stay in the beastly place before one can retire with a large fortune'. The advent of the First World War answered that question once and for all.

In 1912 and 1913, as a result of the Balkan War they had incurred heavy losses. Wheater had backed Mr Bower Ismay's horse, Craiganour, the previous autumn, to win the 1913 Derby. He stood to win £15,000, which was to bolster up the firm's finances, but Cornwallis-West watching the race, saw Craiganour pass the winning post only to be immediately disqualified by the stewards for bumping and boring, although no objection had been raised by the owner, trainer or jockey of the second horse. When the crash came they were in no condition to face a crisis, but inevitably the born gambler managed to save his own skin, leaving his partner with heavy liabilities and no assets.

He told the Official Receiver that since he came of age he had been compelled to raise money to the tune of

£132,000 by mortgages on the reversion of his grand-mother's estates. He admitted the extravagance of himself and his first wife. The estates he would inherit on his father's death were worth £250,000 and he hoped sooner or later to pay all his unsecured debts.

His position had been hopeless from the outset, since his life had changed its direction from the sphere of country gentleman and army officer to that of amateur financier and man about town. In his Edwardian environment, the only stakes were the highest ones.

Among the letters he kept to the end of his life was a four-page one of sympathy and advice written to him at the time of his bankruptcy by Mr Emil Garcke who had welcomed him, years before, onto the board of the British Traction Company.

'You will be a freer man', Garcke wrote 'when it is all over, and the anxiety must have been great, so great to you that a continuance of it would have been impossible to bear. The way you have faced all your troubles has been most courageous and plucky and ought to inspire everyone with admiration for your high character'.

Now trouble of a different kind was brewing.

From the early days of the war much embarrassment had been caused by people writing to Princess Daisy in Germany and to her mother in England begging them to obtain information about relatives through their connexions in these countries. Both responded as best they could and earned for themselves opprobrious labels.

'What people cannot understand they will always suspect', the Princess commented, adding, with slightly faulty logic, that her mother was 'naturally' doing what she could for German prisoners of war in England just as she herself was for English prisoners of war in Germany, and that it laid her open to suspicion and gossip.

In 1916 Patsy Cornwallis-West's folly came to a head on a national scale, causing acute embarrassment and distress to her family and friends.

In addition to interesting herself in German prisoners, from which she had officially to be discouraged, she chose as the object of her solicitude a young sergeant in the Royal Welch Fusiliers, who was recuperating from an illness with a few others at the home of the agent for the West's Welsh estates. The agent's wife looked after the convalescents and took a protective interest in the young man in question who had no home of his own. The Irishwoman evidently saw in him a sensitive and malleable character upon whom she might project her Celtic fantasies and invited him to the Castle. She wanted, she said, to teach him poetry and open his eyes to beauty and romance; she also wanted to remove him from what her riotous imagination conceived to be the clutches of the agent's wife. But the young man, of limited background and deeply religious, felt more at ease in the agent's house, studying for promotion, his claims to which Colonel and Mrs Cornwallis-West had pressed in influential quarters, than in listening to poetry in the emotional atmosphere at the Castle, and, as he feared, offending his God and abusing the Colonel's kindness. He wrote her a letter to that effect and she complained of what she considered his impertinence, to his commanding officer who decided to apply for his transfer out of the neighbourhood and censured him.

Meanwhile the sergeant's promotion to second-lieutenant came through, and also an order for his posting in the normal course of events, which was, however, misconstrued by him and his friends as victimisation. His health suffered, and the agent and his wife took the matter up with a member of parliament. The Cornwallis-Wests appealed to their old friend, Sir John Cowans, Quartermaster-General to the

130

Forces. Representations were made to Lord Kitchener, who dismissed them, but after his death a Court of Inquiry was set up at Mr Lloyd George's instigation, under a specially passed Army Act Amendment Act, to investigate the circumstances of the officer's transfer and the conduct of certain senior officers. In December 1916 the Court's findings were issued in a government report and a week later the contents of the report were published. The Quartermaster-General and other officers were criticised, one was removed from his command, the victim was exculpated and congratulated in the House of Commons by the Under-Secretary of State for War on his vindication, and Mrs Cornwallis-West's behaviour was severely censured. Although the Inquiry had been held in *camera*, names and evidence were made public. *The Times* produced a four-column report and a second leader upholding the castigation.

One voice tried to calm the storm. Her daughter-in-law, Stella, with whom she stayed 'during this time of severe trial for her and for all of us', summed up tersely in a newspaper interview:

I wonder whether the public is aware that Mrs Cornwallis-West is sixty-three years of age, that she is a most impulsive, warm-hearted Irishwoman, one of the most loved of mothers and a dearly loved wife? . . . Surely it is a pitiable affair! I wonder who feels a fine fellow at the end of it? Of one thing I am sure. Nothing will prevent my mother-in-law calling wounded Tommies 'darlings' or alter the poor chance an Irish heart has when it is up against a British middle class one!

A few years after the vociferations of the press had subsided, the sad old story was recorded in more sober tones in the biography of General Sir John Cowans by Desmond Chapman-Huston and Owen Rutter.

What the papers did not. print was the verdict of the

131

people among whom Patsy Cornwallis-West lived her daily life. More than forty years later, when nearly all the main actors in the drama were dead, it was still very much alive in the memory of the people of Ruthin. Everyone I met there brought up 'The Case'. 'There was no harm in it', they insisted, 'no harm. She did it for *a game,* you'd know that if you'd known her'. And a man who had been a young wounded soldier at the time explained: 'If you had come to the hospital to see me, you'd have shaken my hand and asked me how I did, but Mrs Cornwallis-West would have thrown her arms round my neck and kissed me'.

The stationer's daughter summed up the story: 'She was very sentimental and was sorry for the sergeant, and she wanted *for fun* to get him away from the agent's wife, who was a younger woman. She helped to get him a commission, but he upset her and she complained about him and got him into trouble. But when it was all over he came back to live at the agent's and died young'.

At Llanarnon Tower, in its beautiful solitary position on the high hills, the head keeper, who had known them all — Churchills, Plesses, Westminsters, and Mrs Patrick Campbell staying incongruously at the West Arms in the village before she married the heir — pointed down the valley to where the agent's house lay. 'I was in Mesopotamia at the time, but we used to read about the case in the papers sent out from home . . . The old Colonel was a good man, very kind, very quiet, a true country gentleman. When the papers got hold of it, it nearly broke his heart.'

When it was all over the Colonel wrote to his daughter in Germany: 'If you have lately received the English papers you must have read about a certain lady being accused of all sorts of things. Don't believe a word of it, and rest assured from me that the charges are wicked and vile fabrications, and the accusers are vile and vindictive,

132

but they managed to give an entirely wrong impression of what passed . . . The public realise this now and write innumerable letters to her all strongly deprecating the judgment . . . '

When her parents attended a local function in Ruthin soon afterwards they received an ovation.

On a summer day in July 1917 Colonel Cornwallis-West went out after luncheon to smoke a cigar on the terrace at Ruthin, his favourite dog at his feet, his favourite view of the mountains before him. In the sunshine he dozed off, and did not wake again.

'All the town went to his funeral', said John Edwards, who showed me his grave in the New Piece which he had given to enlarge the churchyard. 'The shops were all shut, so that everyone could go. They brought him here on a gun carriage, with the Regimental band, and a hymn in Welsh, and the Last Post.'

A plain headstone bore the inscription 'The desire of a man is in his kindness'.

'He was a Christian gentleman', said my guide, 'a friend of everyone and we loved him. By his lady's wish he was buried the wrong way round — facing west instead of east — so that when he rose again, on the Resurrection morning, the first thing he saw would be the towers of Ruthin, his home'.

IX ❦ The Bright Day Done

To catch up with the affairs of George and Stella it is necessary to go back a little in time.

According to Stella it was she who encouraged her husband to escape from his personal worries by trying his hand at play-writing. He had written a full-length play called 'The Mousetrap' and had asked Shaw for his criticism of it. During 'a fortnight's bliss' at Ruthin, she wrote to Shaw:

> George says you have been so friendly and kind to him . . . Of course the play has amazed me — he has worked on it here and made the love scene stronger — brought the Irish servant into it — it is new — a miracle of fun and feeling — the ease with which George writes and the colour is astonishing. I am grateful he has this talent and I believe it will grow . . . and who knows, perhaps pull up his fortunes a bit.

Shaw, suffering from influenza, replied morosely, 'If you have begun re-writing George's play, God help it and him'. Stella spoke with some insight, for later, when his life was at last on an even keel, he took to writing with great facility, though play-writing remained his least successful medium.

'The Mousetrap' concerned a woman violinist living in the country with her husband. She has social aspirations and longs to go to London. Against his better judgment her husband agrees, and they move there. She is an immediate success and becomes the prey of a professional lady-killer who imagines that the seduction of a country mouse will be easy. On the brink of success he is foiled partly by the husband's best friend and partly by the Irish manservant. A couple of *nouveaux riches* are introduced by way of padding.

To the author's delight, Shaw came and listened to a reading of the play, and a few days later sent him four closely typewritten pages of advice on playwriting.

10 Adelphi Terrace, W.C.
24th March 1916.

My dear Cornwallis-West,

I have one or two things to say about the play for your consideration on Sunday.

Its most serious dramatic defect is that there is only one point of view in it. Now every play ought to have as many points of view as there are characters in it. This defect brings the play to an absolute standstill in the third act. The lady-killer, when the lady repulses him, walks off the stage without a word. This is impossible, both technically and dramatically: to walk out and take no further notice of her would be a victory for him if it were taken as part of the play; if if were not, it would suggest either that the theatre was on fire or that the actor had succumbed to premonitions of a sudden and violent attack of cholera.

His part in the scene must be played from his point of view. He might be genuinely surprised and say 'What an extraordinary woman you are!' Or, if he had Irish habits of speech, he might say brazenly, 'Well, you can't say but you were asked'. Or he might cry, and implore her not to tell her husband, and offer hush money. Or he might be virtuously indignant and threaten to complain to her husband of the way she had led him on. Or he might say that he only did it because he naturally thought she

135

expected him to pay her that compliment, and assure her that her refusal did not break his heart and that he was quite ready to go on being a brother to her. Or, perhaps best of all, he might tell her quite seriously that seducing married women was his chosen occupation in life; that he liked it and was generally successful; and that now he knew she was not that sort of woman they had better shake hands and be friends. The offer of his hand might provoke her to break the Strad over his head, and he might go out laughing on, 'You'll have to explain that broken fiddle, dear lady. So long!' In short there are a dozen ways of getting him off the stage with an exit speech, but not one really effective way of getting him off like a puppet being shovelled into the box when he is done with.

The last act as a whole is open to the objection I mentioned: there is no fresh invention in it: only a harping on what the audience has already seen, with a very unexciting reception of it by the husband. When Geoffrey fails so completely to share his wife's indignation with Jack, he not only becomes a sort of walking sugar stick of kindness and sentimentality but he fails to do what he would do in real life: that is, exasperate her by taking his male friend's part against her, a thing which maddens all wives. Why not follow this up and involve them in a good stiff quarrel, ending in such a dispute as to what actually occurred that, when Jack comes in, it is referred at once to him by both parties? Jack, under cross-examination would of course break down miserably, because he is an imposter who has really seen and heard nothing. Geoffrey would become more and more suspicious; she would become more and more furious; Jack would become more and more involved and more hopelessly convicted by lying; and in the end he would have to confess the truth, and the climax would be the summoning

136

of Larry as the *Deus ex machina* to bring about the happy ending. (Larry might even be driven into declaring he was drunk and invented the whole story; and the two men might accept this with such relief that Molly might decide to pretend that she only kept up the pretence to punish them — what for, God knows, but the audience would take a very thin excuse. There is plenty of material here for a first-rate comedy scene. The act would be tremendously enlivened and you would get rid of that rose painting of your favourite characters which makes the present version too sentimental. Also you would give your man and woman some real acting to do in the last act, instead of sitting there and being too good for this world and talking about what happened in the previous act without giving it any fresh turn.

Indefatigably, Shaw continues:

Another point to be borne in mind is that if you want to preach from the stage, as all great dramatists do, you must have a devil's advocate, or you will inevitably become sententious, like Joseph Surface or the traditional stage sailor who announces that the man who would raise his hand to a woman, save in the way of kindness, is unworthy the name of Briton. This applies to your point about smart society having only one criterion: money. If you want to make that point effectively you must have a scene in which Jack, very sore about it, reproaches somebody for giving him the cold shoulder, and finds that the somebody is quite prepared to defend his position. Zimmerman might be used for this purpose; for as he stands in the existing version he is not a very definite character and would bear further development. His line is obvious enough. 'Well, my dear chap, what other criterion can Society apply? It would be only too willing to be sentimental. It is always talking

137

sentiment, adoring sentiment, playing at sentiment. it asks nothing better than a practical set of Arcadian rules. But the Arcadian rules won't work. The one indispensable qualification for society is to have plenty of money to spend. It is not only disagreeable to know people who are in difficulties, but unkind to themselves to invite them to take part in a routine which they cannot afford. Of course you must not only have money, but must be free of unpresentable relatives, and of the ruder vulgarities: that is why I, Zimmerman, being a foreigner, and therefore having neither relatives in England nor English vulgarities, am accepted where an English manufacturer of my income and standing would find it hard to get in. But now, frankly, would you know me if I had £150 a year? Would you have tolerated me for a moment? You, who have come to my house and drunk my champagne and smoked my cigars and had your whack out of the monstrous sums my wife makes me spend on your class? If not, why should I know you now that you have not even £150 a year, but, as I guess, are a good £1500 to the bad?' That is the way to do it. No conflict: no drama.

Such comedy conflicts will give you a good chance of using your wit and humour, which are too much smothered in your version. Also, you will be able to give yourself away, which is the essence of fine comedy and is indeed the only excuse the playwright has for lecturing or ridiculing his fellow-creatures. There must always be that sort of fair play between the castigator of morals and his audience.

I think the references to kicking and duelling should come out. Suppose we two discovered Carpentier and Jack Johnson offering assignations to Stella and Charlotte, could we do anything but assure them with abject politeness that the ladies were already engaged?

138

Even Othello did not venture to tackle Cassio. The kicking is a melodramatic convention, and a woman has a perfect right to be left open to offers and trusted with her own defence.

I am informed that Stella is in London — that she was seen last night. Disgraceful, I call it.

I go to Ayot tomorrow (Saturday) afternoon and shall not be up until Wednesday or Thursday, except for a few hours on Monday.

Ever
(signed) G. Bernard Shaw

Thirsting for a little old-fashioned praise, Cornwallis-West sent the play to J.M. Barrie, who replied saying nice things about it but denying knowledge of the kind of people portrayed.

I wonder if there are 'persons in Society' to whom money means so much as to swallow up all else, but it may be, and at any rate you make them live and move and have lots of shrewd things to say about them. I am sure it would all act well.

Are there any butlers who drop their h's in this way? I believe you say there are because he is funny, and he is.

Barrie had picked out two points which often bothered other people. In nearly all his fiction-writing Cornwallis-West depicted some of the more unsavoury types in the social scene, upstarts, snobs, go-getters, twisters and spiteful women, 'because they're there,' he would have said, but it puzzled and hurt his friends, who felt that he was gratuitously letting the side down. He loved, too, to write about people in the lower social scale, and to these he allotted a strange mixture of dialects, although he was himself a brilliant mimic of accents and brogues.

He had written a one-act spy play, *Pro Patria,* topical for wartime, which his wife produced and acted in at the

Coliseum early in 1917 and later took on tour to the provinces with some success. It was turned into an opera by Percy Colson and produced by the Carl Rosa Company at the Lyceum Theatre. Colson noted that the author's brilliant and witty wife seemed to revel in making fun of him. ' "Ask George," she would mock, "he knows what is done in *all* best families".' It was a straw in the matrimonial wind.

They could still keep up their act, however, when occasion demanded. Lady Cynthia Asquith, after seeing *The Thirteenth Chair,* in which Mrs Pat was playing, went to her dressing room and 'found her in great spirits. Her happiness has disfigured her as it keeps her fat, but it is wonderful that she should have found it to so great an extent. She calls George West her "golden pheasant"'. On another occasion 'Her young husband came in, and she was terribly arch with him, indulging in shy-making *badinage*. She kissed him on the nose before me'.

Over in France, Stella's son, Alan or Beo (Beloved one), as he was known to his family, was taking a great interest in *Pro Patria* and its author. He too had joined the Royal Naval Division and had taken part with it in the Dardanelles expedition. By the winter of 1916 he was in France, and in almost every letter written to his mother from the trenches there were messages or enquiries about his stepfather.

'Tell George the Ansons did magnificently' (the Anson battalion had been George's own), and in 1917, 'I am so anxious to hear about George's play' and 'Is George better? I met some of his staff in Boulogne recently. . .'

'Do let me know the results of George's play', he kept on writing; evidently the good news did not travel very fast from his mother's pen. 'I am so excited about it . . . I am dying to see him and will write him a play called Beppo and the Brigand.' Beppo was Cornwallis-West's black retriever dog. 'Give him my love, I wish he were here, he would have been a Brigadier by now.'

This attractive if unstable person had apparently found his *métier* in danger. He fought with gallantry in Gallipoli and was mentioned in dispatches, and for action in France received the French Croix de Guerre and the Military Cross with bar early in 1917. His mother did not choose to accompany him to Buckingham Palace to receive it, his wife was no longer 'in the picture'. In Stella's letters there are brief mentions of his American bride, Helen, later the Marchesa Spinola, who was an eye witness of events in the Kensington Square house in the crucial years of 1910 to 1914. She it was who knew all the answers as to what really went on at No. 33 in the years when G.B.S. and G.C-W. were coming and going: they were, as the novelists say, seared on her memory and she disclosed some of them in her recollections, *Nothing But the Truth*. She maintained her friendship with her stepfather-in-law to the end of his life.

'Beo loved George with much affection' his mother admitted. At the end of 1917 he was killed in action in France.

In spite of Stella's optimistic reports to Shaw about her married life, her husband, after his father's death, had applied for a posting to France but was pronounced medically unfit to go overseas again. He was appointed Assistant Provost Marshal to the 57th Division and spent the next two years as A.P.M. for Middlesex and Surrey, occupied with such tiresome jobs as investigating the activities at a houseboat on the Thames where a well-known night club hostess was believed to run a gambling den. Shaw, on hearing the news, remarked that as the Provost Marshal hanged people, he assumed the assistant cut them down.

Perhaps because she could no longer bear its associations

after her son's death, Stella gave up the house in Kensington Square where the most important years of her life had been spent and, early in 1919, rented one in Chelsea where, she told Shaw, there would be room for George's big retriever, ('poor Beppo had gone'), and his sporting gear. She was irritated that he insisted on going on with what she called his 'foolish A.P.M. work', as indeed it was; but it was a job, now more than ever a necessity.

That year he was posted as A.P.M. to the south of Ireland, with headquarters at Cork and a district of seven counties. He was happy to be there again in a military capacity after a gap of twenty-five years, but saddened by what he considered to be the mismanagement of the situation and by the murder of old friends. 'Perhaps soon I'll be going to Cork,' Stella told Shaw in August. 'He writes today he wants me to come.' Did he so write? Now they brought out the worst in each other. The infatuation of 1910 belonged to a vanished world. Any affection which had existed between them had been killed for him by her tantrums and, above all, by her mockery; for her, by his inability to make money or to toe the line to her whims, though her plaint was that he had won her affections by exciting a pity he did not deserve. That his was not a strong character was obvious, but she had had ample time to realise this before she decided to marry him. In Hesketh Pearson's view, 'To love Stella was inevitable, to live with her impossible' and in *The Apple Cart* ten years later Shaw put into the mouth of King Magnus to Orinthia the reason as he saw it:

You see you have never really been married, though you have lead two captives to the altar . . . Being your husband is only a job for which one man will do as well as another . . . being a wife is not your job.

Perhaps the same was true of Cornwallis-West, whom it was difficult to think of as a much-married man and who

142

probably sought in the mature women he married, beyond the flattery of their attraction to him, the security of maternal love.

In February 1920 *Pygmalion* was revived at the Aldwych Theatre with Stella again playing Eliza Doolittle. Later she put out a feeler to Shaw about making a film of it. 'If you let me have *Pygmalion* for the Cinema', she pleaded, 'you will keep me out of the workhouse', getting the dusty answer, 'Alas, alas! nothing will keep you out of the workhouse. All the enchantresses end there'.

She also played the name part that year in a production of *Madame Sand,* by Philip Moëller, looking ravishing in black velvet trousers which drew pained comment from a contemporary playwright, Rudolf Besier, '. . . quite sincerely, they wounded me'.

In July that year Stella and her husband met at the bedside of his mother, though by then their marriage was virtually at an end.

Patsy Cornwallis-West, with her tremendous zest for life, had been defeated by an illness she had kept at bay for two or three years. She spent her last days at Arnewood, the dower house of Newlands, and was buried in the churchyard at Milford where, in the church, are the memorials erected by Theresa West to Mrs Whitby, 'of masculine sense with every feminine charm of person', elegantly sculptured by her daughter, and to Admiral Cornwallis and Captain John Whitby, whos share a vault.

An obituary notice in a Welsh paper recalled, as if to explain all, that she had lived a happy, carefree life in Ireland until she was sixteen, playing about in a tomboyish way without shoes or stockings, before becoming mistress of Ruthin Castle. In Ruthin they had remembered her peals of laughter as she raffled for charity the suit she was wearing and told the winner it wasn't paid for. On such occasions, if the Colonel tried to remonstrate with

143

her, he would begin 'Now, Ma dear,' and he pronounced it 'maw'. 'He *adored* her,' they said.

Her daughter, Daisy, who was closest to her, assessed her thus:

Had she faults or failings? Masses of them . . . She was quick in everything; in thought, speech, repartee, temper, sympathy, likes and dislikes, she seldom let judgment wait upon reflection . . . A woman who could capture and keep as faithful romantic friends such different men as Mr Gladstone and King Edward VII was no ordinary person . . . That she was a good wife and mother one could hardly claim: but she was something rarer. One admires the homely dove, sparrow, robin . . . but one's rapturous love is reserved for the irridescent beauty of the flamingo, kingfisher or peacock.

Her son in his memoirs made no comment at all on his mother beyond a few childhood recollections of her, but one day when he was looking through some old photographs in search of an illustration for a book, he was reminded too poignantly of the terrors of the dark cupboard and of the humiliations suffered by them all through her appalling behaviour. 'My mother was a *wicked* woman!' he exclaimed, and there were tears in his eyes at the memory of old wounds.

In the same year Cornwallis-West applied for his discharge from bankruptcy, it being clear that the creditors would receive twenty shillings in the pound from the proceeds of the sale of the family estates.

He kept for himself only the shooting at Llanarmon, which was let, and a few small collieries. Ruthin Castle suffered 'The Doom of Doolandour' in that it became, after all its vicissitudes, an institution, in fact a hospital and later an hotel. Yet when I visited it the spirit of the recent past still clung to it. Here was 'Mrs Cornwallis-

West's little garden,' there the Ladies' Walk with medie-val heating arrangements, and the underground passages where the children played, and in the private quarters of the house were many Italianate objects which had no doubt been dear to the heart of the Colonel and a curious piece of carving in the butler's pantry under the stairs where Bolton had suffered the invasions from the nursery. The superintendent, the late Dr Sidney Patterson, had fallen under its spell and had devoted his leisure to study-ing its history since early times. As he showed me round, he told me that once, when Cornwallis-West had business at Ruabon, he had revisited his old home and had asked to see a certain room on the second floor. The doctor des-cribed how, as he turned to lead the way his visitor sprang past him, bounding up the stairs two at a time till he reached the door, flung it open and made for the semi-circle of high barred windows with a curved seat below. ' "The bars!" he cried, "they're still there! This was our nursery. This is where we used to stand to see if Moel Fammau was looking glad or sorry".'

The Hampshire estates included valuable arable land, and also coastal property which had been the subject of a well-intentional but, in the end, unsuccessful enter-prise of his father's.

When in 1886 the Colonel became entitled to a life-holding of the Hampshire properties entailed on his son, he obtained an Order in the Court of Chancery appointing three Trustees to have charge of the money obtained for any land, he himself to receive only the interest. He then set about developing the land about Hordle Cliff as a sea-side resort, somewhat on the lines adopted by another private landowner, the Duke of Devonshire, at Eastbourne.

There were splendid views both eastward and westward and the beach extended for miles. Behind the gorse-covered cliffs, the new building estate of Milford-on-Sea

145

was envisaged and, in those days, rapidly proceeded with. The Hotel Victoria was built, and Cornwallis, Whitby and Pless Roads made, followed by others with family names, Headfort and De La Warr. The Duke of Devonshire's landscape gardener was paid £100 for a one-day visit to draw up a grandiose plan for amenities which subsequently proved to be impractical.

In the eighteen-nineties Colonel Cornwallis-West and his trustees handed over his interests to a body of residents who were prepared to subscribe annually towards the maintenance of the new resort, he agreeing to double the amount subscribed. This scheme proved too costly, and after ten years the committee handed back its responsibilities to the Colonel, who was unable to find any public body to take it over. For although Haldanes and Abercorns, Asquiths and Tennants patronised the hotel, there were no man-made amusements to attract visitors in any numbers, nor was the drainage system adequate.

He had wished to create something more than an ordinary seaside resort: it was to be a select, well-planned and artistic one. This he tried to do by first allowing only one house on a plot of half to one acre, next by regulating the value of the house to be built, which was to be not less than £1,200, and thirdly he insisted that the plans of each house should be approved by himself or his architect. An anticipation of town and country planning?

In 1920 all the properties comprising the Newland Estates were put up for sale, but the Parish Council of Milford was eventually enabled to buy the seafront and foreshore rights.

Incredibly, as it must have seemed to those who knew her, Jennie Churchill died in 1921 from the effects of a fall. A few years earlier she had been married for the third time to Montagu Porch, son of a west country landowner

146

and, fittingly, somewhat of an adventurer. By coincidence his surname was familiar to her for when, in South Africa, she had obtained leave to go up to see the front at Chievely Camp, the small party that had accompanied her had included, as she noted, 'last but not least, the coxswain of the *Terrible,* Porch by name'. After Cambridge and the Boer War Montagu Porch had worked with Sir Flinders Petrie in Egypt, had collected antiquities in the Sinai Desert and organised the building of the first town in Nigeria. When he met Lady Randolph while on leave in Rome in 1914 he was thirty-seven, she sixty. They corresponded, and later he joined her on a visit to her sister, Lady Leslie, at Glaslough. They were married in June 1918.

According to the comments he permitted himself to make in an interview for the press some forty years later it was, characteristically, Lady Randolph who determined they should marry, saying 'You know I could never marry a man of my own age'. They realised some people might be censorious of their marriage: did they care? 'Care?' the old gentleman is reported to have said, 'I was in love. Just say she was very human . . . and made me supremely happy'.

They lived in her last home in Westbourne Street, close to Hyde Park, and Queen Alexandra, with whom she had played duets in the seventies, used to come to tea.

There are glimpses of her during the war years through the admiring eyes of Edward Marsh, arranging luncheons, as she always had done, for Winston to meet interesting people, or working at a hospital as, in the words of Siegfried Sassoon who was a patient, 'a sort of Olympian head matron', or giving an Armistice supper party.

The obituary notice in *The Times* described her as 'a brilliant and high-stepping figure who flung herself ardently into many occupations: literature, hunting, drama, politics,

147

marriage . . . To the last, no illness, no social change, could dim her courage and kindliness'.

That kindliness could have no better illustration than the letter she had written to her ex-husband two years previously:

My dear George,

 I heard all about you from Clare . . . I am glad you wrote . . . and in your heart of hearts you must know that I never could have any but kindly feelings towards you. I never think of you but to remember all those happy days we spent together . . . I have forgotten everything else. I do wish you all that is best . . . Peace is an essential to life and if you have that you are on a fair way to happiness. Life is frightfully hard. One's only chance is within oneself . . . Bless you . . . Always your best friend,

Jennie.

Further light is shed on her character by the book of essays she published in 1916, *Small Talks on Big Subjects*. Although they make rather trite reading now — they were very much of their period — the sentiments were the writer's own: the Girl of Today, Friendship, Suffragist Strategy, Personality, The Peace that War Begets, are some of the eighteen titles. The essay on Personality is interesting in the light of her son's development:

Whatever the definition, the general idea of a personality is one who adheres to his own beliefs, rightly or wrongly, and to his own mode of life, without fear or respect of his surroundings . . .

She cites the outstanding force of Gladstone's personality and the dangerously persuasive charm of Arthur Balfour.

The great secret of personality is the power of giving oneself — if there is anything to give . . . Without it the front rank can never be reached . . . its complete fulfilment is only possible where it is combined with the power to achieve and attain.

On Extravagance, a subject on which she was well qualified to speak, she wrote:

Women as a rule are capable of as great self denial as men, but their upbringing is different, and not habitually having the responsibility of money they are content . . . merely to have the spending of an allowance which is often elastic.

Characteristically, the last essay in the book is on Forms of Excitement, and the last words:

The most thrilling, and perhaps the most worthy form of excitement, is that which comes from within — created in the soul of man, and not by any exterior agency. Such excitement is known to all who do good work, who see it grow out of their labour and their inspiration.

One can imagine her son's voice speaking the words. In her autobiography she had quoted Pearl Craigie's reminder to her of 'the words of the immortal Mrs Chick to Florence Dombey. "If any misanthrope were to put in my presence the question 'Why were we born?' I should reply, To make an effort" '. It could have been her own motto.

For the next few years George and Stella moved restlessly about on their separate ways. He never returned to her and she avenged herself by keeping him legally bound to her for the rest of her life. It was not until December 1921 that she apparently told Shaw her version of their story, wanting, as she said, his 'clever opinion how to get just enough truth on the written page. I thought you knew he left me two years ago'; but Shaw, whose sympathies were with George as they would have been with any husband of Stella's, managed for the next twenty years to balance on a knife-edge of neutrality between them. He listened to Stella's diatribes and to George's plaints and with his huge understanding of human nature was able to laugh gently at them and to pity them.

She had retired to Lancashire to write her autobiography and to carry on her tantalising arguments with G.B.S., uttering by turns pleas and threats to secure his permission to include, in the face of all his counter-imprecations and cajolings, the inflammatory letters which he had written to her in 1912-13 at the height of his literary passion. In the end she did just that, though 'His wildest letters I do not give' she murmurs, in her book. *My Life and Some Letters,* published in 1922, was a medley in somewhat emotional tones of personal and theatrical history interspersed with letters from her family and the famous. As Desmond MacCarthy gracefully said of it, 'She has tilted the shafts of memory's cart and let the contents fall. There they lie . . .' and there was drama enough between the lines.

On returning to London to receive the bouquets it brought her from the many illustrious names mentioned in it, she stayed at various homes offered her by friends. '. . . I arrived in this horses house on Saturday. Mrs Benjamin Guinness has let it to me cheaply', was a typical gibe from an address in Carlton Mews.

Stories about Stella in these later years are legion. Some unpublished recollections reached me from a woman journalist of the twenties who had visited her for an interview in the Guinness home at Carlton House Terrace. Mrs Campbell was not at all dressed for the interview and the caller received a slipper at her head. A few months later, however, she was invited to tea in Pont Street, and for two hours, in a room where the mantelpiece had been painted by her 'kindly benefactress', again Mrs Guinness, Mrs Pat improvised a play, enthrallingly, for her benefit.

At a dinner party she gave, the guests admired the ex-

150

quisite Venetian glass which adorned the table. The next day it vanished like the treasure in Aladdin's cave, for, ever resourceful, she had ordered a wide range of specimens on approval. Having been used for the party, they were returned with some excuse to the store which had loaned them. Yes, the manager said, they knew about the dinner party, but it was better policy to give way to Mrs Campbell than to make an enemy of her.

'The French use the word *méchant*', wrote my correspondent. 'She was born that way. And she was her own worst enemy. Masses of people helped her and got nothing for their pains, — she always bit the hand of kindness — and yet one was struck dumb in her presence, there was something so majestic, so awe-inspiring . . . One never knew what she would do next . . . she was extremely kind to me of course, as her next meal often depended on what I wrote about her'.

'How gifted she was at knowing how to upset somebody', remarked the actress Athene Seyler in a broadcast retrospect, and years previously Mrs Lyttelton had commented on her attitude to other people in the theatre: '. . . she has no motive but merely a succession of violent antipathies and prejudices and contempts with moreover ignorance added, i.e. she is quite unable to teach or to build up another person's talent — she can only destroy and that is why she is fatal as a producer. She as Mr Barker very truly says "subtly humiliates and disconcerts people". She does not set out to do this — it just arises from the inevitable impact of her dominating personality'.

Cornwallis-West, back from Ireland and retired from the army, went through a bad period. For the first time in his life he found himself homeless and jobless. He applied for many appointments, but there were other demobilised officers of his age and younger on the same quest, and the testimony of commanding officers, 'most conscientious', 'very good disciplinarian', 'capable organiser', 'instilled law and order into a turbulent Irish crowd by his personality' carried no magic then.

Before his mother's death he had gone through with her the papers stored at Newlands, where his grandmother and aunts had apparently kept every letter ever written to them. It was then that the Landor letters were thrown away, but he recognised as important the naval papers of Admiral Cornwallis which, in boxes methodically labelled by the old sailor, had remained undisturbed since his death, apart from a bequest by Mrs West to Cornwallis Wykeham Martin and the loan of one box in 1898 for the purpose of the Navy Record Society's publication *The Blockade of Brest*.

Although compelled to let the papers go for sale, he determined to make literary use of the naval history and the human story they contained, as a tribute to the original owner of the home they had all loved.

X ❧ *The Gentle Interlude*

There is a gap of ten years in the correspondence with Shaw, from 1916 to 1926. Undaunted by Shaw's criticism of his first play, Cornwallis-West had, since parting from Stella, been working on another in which he attempted to depict the erratic temperament of an artist and the impossibility of making such a character happy in private life. It was called 'Some Do and Some Don't' and its chief characters were an Irish baronet, his mother, and a famous star in grand opera, supported by the latter's devoted and down-trodden secretary and Sir Paul's Irish manservant. In the opening scene Paul reads in the paper the announcement of his engagement to Myra, the singer. His mother forces him to admit that he is taken aback and had not authorised it. He swears her to secrecy and refuses to contradict the announcement. Six months later he and Myra, now married, are already the subject of the servants' gossip because of their rows. The scenes worked up by the leading lady are evidently the breath of life to her, and the bickerings have a familiar ring.

'Why do you always take the part of the servants?' Myra complains. When Paul remarks that he and she are not putting up a very good show, she shudders. 'What a common way you have of expressing yourself! . . . you offend me.' There are threats and tears and always a reconciliation — until the next time. The play ends with their parting.

He sent it off to Shaw, whose reply has, as a manuscript,

an especial interest as it is throughout in a handwriting which at first glance is not unlike Shaw's own. The late Miss Blanche Patch, Shaw's secretary for thirty years, identified it for me as that of Mrs Shaw. She wrote:

> I have studied the letter carefully and have come to the conclusion that it was written by Charlotte [Mrs Shaw] and dictated to her by GBS from his sick bed.
>
> He never had a secretary at Ayot and I, who went to him in 1920, would have been at Adelphi Terrace in 1926 . . . When I wrote answers to Shaw's letters I generally began 'Mr Shaw requests me to say so-and-so' and signed them in my own name. The 'pp. G. Bernard Shaw' is, I am sure, in Charlotte's writing.

She enclosed a letter of Mrs Shaw's so that I could see for myself that the hands were identical, as indeed they were.

Ayot St Lawrence, Welwyn, Herts.
7 March 1926

Dear Cornwallis-West,

I got the play all right at Falmouth and read it; but I was far behind with my correspondence even then and have fallen further and further into arrear. I am now, finally, landed in bed with an avalanche of work.

The play is not at all uninteresting as a character sketch but I should not produce it if I were a manager, not because it is in any way unpresentable as a piece of work, but because the attempt to present that particular character on the stage has been made, by Haddon Chambers and others, even including lately St J. Ervine; and it has never been successful, for a reason that ought to be obvious enough though somehow it escapes notice until too late.

That reason is that if a person has an entirely peculiar, idiosyncratic unaccountable fascination, as a result of which she becomes hopelessly spoilt, and un-

154

bearable in all the ordinary relations of life, the only thing you can put on the stage is the unbearable part, with the fascination omitted. One contemplated Haddon Chambers' lady, and said, 'This is an odious woman; why the devil dont they kick her out of the house. What interest is there in her vagaries? And why do they go on pretending that she is charming and irresistible and that we must forgive her everything she does, when, as a matter of fact she is neither charming nor irresistible nor have we the slightest inclination to forgive her anything; quite the contrary?'

I think that is the whole case against the play. It is a pity because your heroic sacrifice of yourself as the lady's victim struck me as extraordinarily funny. But in fact, the real centre of the play ought to be the hero not the heroine; it is the comedy of his escape rather than the tragedy of his capture which offers the real material for an attractive bit of work.

Ever

pp. G. Bernard Shaw.

Sec.

In his memoirs Cornwallis-West named the play by Haddon Chambers as *The Impossible Woman.* This was an adaptation from the novel, *Tante,* by Anne Douglas Sedgwick (Mrs Basil de Sélincourt) and he was careful to mention that the plot of his own play was conceived 'on lines somewhat similar to *Tante* where a man falls a victim to the fatal fascination of an irresistibly charming but temperamentally difficult woman': a discreet piece of camouflage against the possible criticism that he had used too blatantly his own domestic situation.

St John Ervine's play, *Mary, Mary, Quite Contrary,* a variation on the same theme, had been produced at the Savoy Theatre the previous summer and was, its author agreed, undoubtedly the play of his that Shaw had in mind.

George Grossmith, who also read the play, wrote:

It is so particularly well written that I wish the story were more worth while. The character of Myra is a fine study, but . . . it seems to me that to compete with the 'Movies', plays and stories must move quickly and give the public little time to think.

In May 1926 there occurred the interlude of the General Strike which gave him another chance to drive a train. He volunteered at Paddington and drove Great Western Railway trains throughout the emergency.

A *Daily Telegraph* article written on his experiences during the strike evoked, to his delight, a letter of congratulation from the now retired engine driver, Charles Day, who had given him his first lessons on a locomotive. Day recalled that once, at the beginning of the Boer War, he had driven a train, with Field Marshal Lord Methuen and General Gatacre in a saloon carriage next to the engine, from Waterloo to Southampton, where on the platform were Colonel and Mrs Cornwallis-West, 'and the Colonel shouted to me, "Well, Charlie, we've sent George over to Kruger!" '

In the last few years Cornwallis-West had made the Guards Club his base and had spent much of his time in the country looking after the children of a dead friend. The youngest, a baby girl, was made his ward. He enjoyed teaching them to ride and fish and train dogs, but when at last his affairs were settled and he knew that a modest income remained to him, he looked around for a home of his own. The house he found was in a quiet side street off Montpelier Square.

No. 8 Sterling Street had six small rooms on three floors, a basement and a balcony. In it he made a miniature museum of furniture, pictures and china, but also a comfortable home. In the dining room were the Adam tea caddies, the Georgian porringers, the water colours of Ruthin, the Hoppner and Raeburn family portraits and a picture of Captain Whitby's ship. Upstairs in the study, Crown Derby pot-pourri urns flanked the French clock on the mantelpiece, miniatures mounted on black velvet hung above it, the cartoon of his father by Spy beside the fireplace. A Lorenzo Lotto nativity glowed from the wall between the tall windows; a cluster of pale gold seals used by his father lay on the desk with the ormolu ink-stand. On one Sheraton side table were the oriental chessmen and the ivory backscratcher, and on its twin the Edwardian trinkets, the snuff boxes, and a massive set of cameo jewellery given by George III to an ancestor at his court.

Beside the tapestry firescreen stood the sculptured head of a girl, by Emil Fuchs, on a green marble pedestal. Arab sketches by Rex Ingram as they sat together in a Tunis café were on the bookcase, and everywhere photographs of the beautiful women who had played a part in his life peopled the room. Granny Olivia, in a lace shawl, Patsy, with ermine cap and muff in an artificial snowstorm, his sisters, Shelagh in regal gown and court feathers, Daisy, by Sargent, and Jennie with the diamond aigrette in her hair, all were there. Only Stella was missing.

In the basement an admirable gentleman's gentleman-cum-butler-cum-chauffeur, with his wife, a cordon bleu cook, gave him perfect service and devotion.

Having acquired a home he turned his attention to the Cornwallis papers and wrote a series of articles on them for *The Daily Telegraph*. The interest these evoked prompted him to write a full-scale biography of the Admiral.

The Life and Letters of Admiral Cornwallis covered its subject's career from midshipman to admiral; his participation in the War of American Independence and the wars with France and Spain between 1777 and 1785; his command of the East India Squadron from 1789 to 1793 and his command of the Channel Fleet during the threat of Napoleonic invasion. It included the rise, victories and death of Nelson, whose friendship with the Admiral dated from the time when Cornwallis had saved his life by bringing him home in his ship *Lion* in 1780, 'so emaciated' that it was doubted whether he would survive.

Admiral of the Fleet Lord Beatty wrote a foreword, ending: 'Major Cornwallis-West has performed a public service in writing the life of this great sailor, and I commend his pages to those who take pride in the history of our country and in the Navy in which Cornwallis rendered such noble service'. After reading the published work he supplemented his remarks with an enthusiastic four-page letter.

The book told a fascinating and authentic story in excellent prose, but with the ill-luck that attended its author's every venture, the publishing firm to whom he had entrusted it went into liquidation almost immediately, and he received nothing but the congratulations of those who read it.

He was invited by Lord Burnham to continue his articles in *The Daily Telegraph* in the form of Edwardian reminiscence, related where possible to the current social or sporting events of the week, and these he contributed for the next few years. He also began, by way of light relief after the biography, to write a novel.

Thinking back to the time when I first visited the house and later got to know its routine, I remember it as a happy one, run at concert pitch. At the top of the stairs where the study was, Dawn, a spaniel on a visit from the country, panted in an ecstasy of anticipation as to what might happen next; below stairs Campbell pressed and polished with his black coat at the ready, knowing that if the study bell rang from the first floor, his master would also come out on to the landing with a fine bellow in the belief that he was saving his man's legs. Through the open windows a piano rippled continuously in the house across the road where the Danish ladies lived; in late summer the penetrating cry of the lavender sellers broke the silence of the sunny street. Old friends up from the country for Wimbledon or holiday shopping, Elweses from Gloucestershire, Porters from Pershore, Calleys and Cartwrights came and went. There were jokes and laughter and talk of Orpen and John and newer talents at the Royal Academy, of Gielgud and young Olivier, Evans and Ashcroft, the rising talent of the serious stage, of Priestley's latest comedy and of the stars who scintillated on the concert platform and in the opera during these years.

Because of his tireless energy, disciplined by military training, every minute of the day was filled. Reading the papers, answering letters, writing in the morning; luncheon at one-thirty or, if the mayfly were rising, a dash to the nearest river, the Hertfordshire Lea, with some mutton pies in the haversack and some proofs to read while waiting for the trout to rise ('the fish keep God's time' he used to say when the clocks were altered for Summer Time); back to tea, in theory at least, a walk to the Turf Club for a game of bridge till seven or so; home to bath and change in exactly twenty minutes and to emerge, meticulously groomed, in a faint aura of eau-de-cologne and a glow of anticipation for whatever the evening held: dinner at the house of friends or at home with two or three guests, followed by a play or the opera or the latest film.

An incident comes back to me. I hear the familiar sound of a taxi drawing up — he did not use Chrissie the Chrysler for short journeys — the ping of its bell, the chink of small change spinning down the gutter from a disgruntled driver (the deprived child remains mean about little things): then he bounded up the stairs two at a time with an armful of violets. An old Irish crone had waylaid him in the street with a hard luck story and he had bought her entire stock and sent her off to comfort herself with 'a dhrap o' the cratur'. The flowers belied their lavish appearance, for when I looked closely at them I saw that they were almost dead.

He kept in touch with Shaw, sometimes on the subject of plays, and, more particularly, on Stella's refusal to put an official end to their marriage. He would have liked very much to entertain G.B.S. in the peaceful atmosphere of his own home, and in the next letter Shaw is evidently wriggling on the pin of a pressing invitation to dine in Sterling Street, with the inducement that the perfect cook would bring all her artistry to bear on a menu appropriate to his vegetarian taste.

4 Whitehall Court, London, S.W.1.
2nd July 1928.

My dear G. C-W.

I can no more dine out than I can answer letters when it is humanly possible to postpone them. As we are off to the South of France on the 15th, and preparations for the trip will fill up the few days I shall spend in London in the meantime, I must cry off until I come back to England sometime in September. Then perhaps we can fix something. After all, your cook is as good for lunch as for a dinner.

Being a sympathetic man you will understand that I must not remind my family circle of Stella more than I can help. That confounded book made it a sore subject.

As Lady A evidently had no idea of the irrevocability of the rupture between you and S, I, after thinking it over, showed her your letter. It carried conviction.

How S manages to live I don't know. If all her friends were to give her all they possess it would last her about three weeks. And she has made a devil of a lot of enemies.

> Ever
>
> G.B.S.

Many thanks for the book. It makes a queer old story. What a lot they were!

The 'confounded book' was, of course, Stella Campbell's autobiography. Shaw was always extremely anxious to spare his wife's feelings, albeit sometimes in a rather ostrich-like way, but Charlotte Shaw remained inordinately sensitive and was never really able to adjust herself, in this context, to being a great man's wife.

'Lady A', Shaw's great friend, Viscountess Astor, M.P., was among Stella's benefactors. With her reforming zeal she may have believed that Shaw could be instrumental in bringing George and Stella together again.

The book referred to in the postscript was *The Life and Letters of Admiral Cornwallis.* Shaw would have little patience and less respect for some of the curious goings-on of the admirals.

He knew by experience, quite as well as Cornwallis-West, Stella's incorrigible attitude towards money and kindnesses, and continually chided her about it. A short letter from him a year later reports in rather cryptic language an attempt at negotiation with her, to which he has added his own ironic twist. The bidding for a divorce had begun.

> 4 Whitehall Court, London S.W.1.
>
> 27th June 1929.

Dear G. C-W.

I mentioned the matter in the course of a reply to a letter about other things, stressing the precariousness of the literary profession and the legal obligation of the wives of literary men to support them. This ingenious inversion of the risks of the situation elicits the unruffled remark 'You must not believe all that George says', and nothing more. However, the facts have their own weight and will no doubt sink in by themselves.

Ever

G.B.S.

The debate continued, and six months later Cornwallis-West received a splendidly Shavian report on the stalemate in the negotiations, for relations between Shaw and Stella had again been strained. In the spring of 1929 Shaw had completed his new play, *The Apple Cart,* which had its first performance in Warsaw and was to be produced in England by Sir Barry Jackson at the Malvern Festival, with Edith Evans in the part of Orinthia, the Egeria of King Magnus. Mrs Campbell, when she first heard of it, hoped to play the part herself, but later she learned, through a chance meeting with Miss Evans and the reconnaissances of her friend, Mrs Alfred Lyttelton, that Orinthia had been modelled on her own personality, and was indignant. Nervously Shaw wrote to her that he did not know whether she would like it or not. She left him in no doubt: for he had tried to paint as true a picture of her fascination and her inconsistencies, her wheedlings and her tantrums, as any author could hope to do. He made a few changes to humour her and tried to reassure her:

Orinthia's husbands are not Patrick or George; they are items in the many millions of men and women, who, seduced by a splendour that dazzles them, bite off more than they can digest . . . Do you not know that though you are marvellous . . . you are gey ill to live with; indeed impossible.

She retaliated by threatening to sell the letters he had written to her, and was not mollified by his expressions

162

of admiration for her acting in *The Matriarch*, the play of Jewish life by G.B. Stern, in which she had considerable success and a good run. Seeing her myself, for the only time, in this play, I recall a memorably tyrannical figure, with a deep contralto voice, making a marvellous entrance, in a wheel chair, draped in shawls and clutching a forbidden ham to her bosom; or transforming a dingy room, with a flourish of cushions and covers, into an exotic place.

4 Whitehall Court, London,S.W.1.
16th Jany 1930.

Dear C-W.,

You don't suppose I have any choice in the matter of lunches, do you? I go like a lamb where I am taken, much in the manner of King Magnus.

You know how crochety Orinthia is about money: how, for instance, she insists on being paid in odd halfpence for matinees even when the alternative is to be paid more to include them in her weekly salary. Well, she considers you owe her a sum of — I forget* it, but think it is either £6400 or £4600 — for debts etc. paid by her when the household broke up. I demonstrated in the manner of an accountant that taking this sum plus compound interest as due to her last year, £800 a year would much more than cover the interest on it. But she is not accessible to accountancy; and as the success of The Matriarch took the strain off the financial situation, nothing further passed to my knowledge. And since the Apple Cart (I read the scene to her and altered a few strokes to please her). I have not heard from her, less, I fear, on the play's account than on that of the fifteen years which have transformed me into a bore in the fashion of the Ancient Mariner.

I am delighted to hear of the success of Two Lives.

* Against this line is a pencilled note 'lies G. C-W.'

163

If you can keep that up you are a made man. Hold on to your film rights like an octopus.

Ever

G.B.S.

The mention of £800 a year in this context suggests that, as her husband had recently sold his last remaining property in Wales, it was a proposition for alimony should she agree to give him his freedom.

Writing later to Frank Harris about *The Apple Cart*, Shaw told him:

> For some time before the War I was on much the same intimate terms with Mrs Campbell as King Magnus with Orinthia . . . Yet I was as faithful a husband as King Magnus; and his phrase 'our strangely innocent relations' is true.

When, after the success of Hesketh Pearson's biography of him, there was a suggestion to make a screen version of his life, his comment was:

> The Interlude in *The Apple Cart* does all that can be done on the stage with myself and Stella Pat Campbell:
> . . . All other attempts to put Stella on the stage have been ghastly failures.

The pendant to Letter No. 6 is an inscription in the Christmas present which Shaw sent to Cornwallis-West at the end of this year, and so I quote it now. In a copy of the printed edition of *The Apple Cart: A Political Extravaganza* (Constable, London, 1930), he wrote:

To George Cornwallis West

from George Bernard Shaw

25th Dec. 1930.

You will appreciate the Interlude

We are Initiates.

Shaw's reference to 'Two Lives' was a mistake for *Two Wives*, Cornwallis-West's first novel, which was published by Putnams in London and New York in December 1929

164

in time to send as a Christmas present. Its theme was suggested to him by Rex Ingram's having asked him, during a conversation in Nice, for a film plot involving self sacrifice. The novel told a simple, sentimental story of the love of a young Frenchwoman, Antoinette, for a good-hearted Englishman, Tony, who had gone to Blois to learn French as a preliminary to entering diplomacy. Into the plot he introduced, as he was fond of doing, types from a social setting different from his own, a middle-class French girl, a parvenu knight, his homely wife and spoilt daughter, and a society woman who had been 'nobody in particular'.

It was to be called 'Tony and Toinette' and so, up to the page-proof stage it was. Then the publishers suggested he should call it *Two Wives*. Cornwallis-West revolted. His hero had married the wrong girl and after many tribulations married the right one, and to put the emphasis on the two marriages rather than on the star-crossed lovers was in his view to upset the balance of the story. In the end the gentle persuasion of Mr Huntington of Putnam's won, on the grounds that they knew best what was likely to attract sales. Those who hoped to find in it any obvious autobiographical revelations were disappointed, though in the society woman's bickerings with her well-born husband there is the familiar sound of life with Stella: 'He had fallen in the first instance to her physical charms and when these became stale had come positively to dislike her wife. He loathed rows and she loved them'.

The book was dedicated to his sisters and was re-published in America in 1930. It was typical of Shaw, ever practical, to give the author a reminder about holding on to his film rights, though in fact the film never materialised. Letters he received from readers as far away as Australia complimented him on his characterisation. Emil Garcke, his old friend and employer, writing of this 'entrancing book,' likened the character of 'Toinette to Rachel in Dickens's *Hard Times,* and Daisy, seriously ill in her villa near Cannes, wrote:

> Oh, Buzzie darling, I have just finished your delightful book . . . Buzzie boy, it was charming, a book full of true nature and no acting. Oh how I wish you could have married a wife like 'Toinette, someone young whom you could have taught life and love to, and had dear little children whom you would have loved.

He did at this rather late stage in his life believe that he would very much like to marry 'someone young' if he could get his freedom, but as he was so happy in his un-encumbered, bachelor-like existence it may be that the illusion was more precious to him than the reality might have been.

As soon as the novel was in the press Cornwallis-West began his next book. The popularity of his articles in *The Daily Telegraph* had brought the suggestion from his publishers and others that he should write his memoirs, and so, reluctantly, because he was now set on story-telling and full of ideas for plots, he agreed to do so. He chose the apt title, *Edwardian Hey-Days,* but because of the book's diversity he insisted on the sub-title *A Little About a Lot of Things,* which met the possible criticism that its range was too wide to be deep.

He was careful to consider the feelings of people still living. He had included a story of Caruso gargling on the stage while singing in opera with Melba, and sent her a proof-cutting for approval. She replied immediately, re-living the part in *Rigoletto* as she wrote:

> My dear George . . . Please cut it all out . . . I do not remember the incident in the last act — I am not near the tenor, there is a wall between him and me as I am with my father. I liked Caruso — so kind to everyone . . .

Needless to say, the offending passage was removed, though the comment of one of Melba's biographers, Percy

Colson, lends colour to the anecdote: 'I never met a singer who was so fussy about his health as was Caruso . . . His dressing-room was like a chemist's shop, so full was it of sprays, douches, pastilles, gargles and throat remedies of every kind'.

The book was published by Putnam in 1930, in an olive green, William Morris type of binding with a dust jacket of Morris's elegant willow-leaf wallpaper design. If it brought to his friends happy and humorous memories, it must equally have disappointed readers who had hoped for some period scandals.

Sir Harold Nicolson, devoting to it a double-column review in *The Evening Standard,* had this to say:

Here we have a jolly book . . . The whole Edwardian era lives in that phrase, 'One or two hostesses,' 'all the Rothschilds,' — no, it cannot be bettered . . . In reading Mr Cornwallis-West's outright memoirs, I pause for a moment and think, yes, this is true and vivid. And yet there was something more in it than ostentation.

He went on to define the virtues of the Edwardian epoch in two words — 'concentration and conviction . . . Today we render to God the things that are Caesar's with a flabby puggy hand . . .'

His old friend Cyril Drummond wrote from Cadland expressing the opinion shared by other contemporaries who respected the author for his reticence though there was the occasional complaint that the book told a lot about the field sports the author engaged in but little about the women he married. The fact that he did not gossip about his wives speaks for itself.

A copy was sent to Shaw as a Christmas present, and a card came back by way of temporary reply.

Ayot St Lawrence, Welwyn, Herts.

5th January 1931.

Thanks for the book: I have only half devoured it as

yet: it is in some demand here.

I have only two days in town this week after 3 weeks absence; and they are crammed with deferred engagements: your suggestion of a pleasant hour to ourselves elicits nothing but a hollow laugh.

More when I finish the book and have a moment to discuss things.

G.B.S.

Shaw had now adopted a stylised form of a signature running his initials together with a long 3″ - 4″ flourish cutting diagonally through them. It is used on all the remaining letters quoted, except those with a full signature.

No mention of Stella: the coolness between them after *The Apple Cart* affair lasted for some time and the published letters show no communication between them during the year 1930, but quite apart from the subject of Stella, Cornwallis-West longed for the elixir of an hour of Shaw's company.

It is not surprising that Shaw's next letter on the negotiations which were still being relentlessly pressed on him, by one side or the other, was a guarded one. A proposal that might be construed as collusive had been implied in the letter of 16 January 1930.

4 Whitehall Court, London, S.W.1.
10th May 1931.

My dear G. C-W.,

On reflection it is clear to me that the lady has been soundly advised as to the need for avoiding any proposal that could be construed as collusive, and has left any sort of reciprocity to be inferred.

I am writing to her by this post, and will let you know the result, if any.

G.B.S.

Shaw evidently addressed his letter to Stella in America,

where she frequently stayed in the late twenties and thirties hoping to get film work, but by June she was back in England, in intransigent mood, still threatening to sell his letters.

His next communication to Cornwallis-West was brief but pithy:

4 Whitehall Court, London, S.W.1.

4th June 1931.

My letter, I presume, was returned to America. Apparently what is wanted is a confession. Why not make one 5,000 words long?

G.B.S.

The card on which it was written was presumably accompanied by her latest letter, for her husband to see and return.

Stella's love for George, if it ever existed, had certainly turned to hatred. She wanted a full confession of 'crimes', which he was ignorant of having committed. For now she sought to put on him the sole responsibility for the failure of their marriage, disturbed, perhaps, by the thought that future generations might see her not as a misused woman but in the chameleon-like character of Orinthia.

Encouraged by the reception of his memoirs, and by the requests he received from fellow sportsmen for more of his experiences, Cornwallis-West now occupied himself with producing a book on his favourite sport, fishing. As it was to be a companion to *Edwardian Hey-Days* in reminiscent vein, he did not overburden it with technicalities, but merely introduced 'here and there a few useful hints to my younger readers for attaining proficiency in "the gentle art", trusting that the older ones will say nothing about "sucking eggs" ', It was called *Edwardians Go Fishing: or Many Days on Many Waters,* and was published in 1932. I quote from the 'Envoi' for what it tells about

169

the man.

These reminiscences have been a joy to write, for they have conjured up so many happy memories. Memories of lovely rivers meandering through fields golden with cowslips and marsh marigolds, of glorious days with fleecy clouds and flitting swallows and battles with speckled trout; memories of icy blasts in March, when the tugs and rushes of silvery salmon made up for all discomfort; and, above all, memories of good fellowship and of friends . . . To those who are left . . . I dedicate a new 'Fisherman's Prayer':

> Pray God still grant me many a day
> On many lakes and many streams
> Pray God the monsters that I slay
> May be realities, not dreams.
>
> Pray God that if a fish is lost
> I do not break my rod in half;
> And that, no matter what the cost,
> I do not curse but still can laugh.
>
> When Time can be no more defied,
> Dear Lord, this is my final wish
> When I have put my rod aside,
> To gaze into the fire — and fish!

By the time the fishing book was out he was already at work on a new novel and also a play. He had a wonderfully fertile imagination for the invention of plots, and with practice and discipline his stories might have become best-sellers, but success in the theatre was what he still coveted. His light three-act comedy, *The Methods of Margot,* centred on a middle-aged wooing, was written with Yvonne Arnaud in mind, and there is a note from her expecting the play to be sent to her by Ronald Squire, but no indication that it ever reached her. It was, however, sent to Marie Tempest, another obvious choice for the lead, and her husband W. Graham Browne, himself an experienced actor, replied:

It is a very amusing play. My only doubt is that it may be too light. It would have done very well at the Criterion and I think I should have done it if I had got it a year or so ago; but the Haymarket is a much bigger theatre and they seem to expect more for the same money. I have sent it to my manager . . .

I congratulate you on a neat, cheery and at times very funny little comedy.

Eventually it was presented at the Q Theatre by Jack de Leon, and produced by Matthew Forsyth.

This time Cornwallis-West had not sent the play to Shaw but waited until he could tell him that it was being rehearsed, then hopefully suggested that he should come to a rehearsal. Hence this reply:

4 Whitehall Court, London, S.W.1.
11th May 1933.

Dear George

You are up against professional etiquette in this matter. I can't go to another producer's rehearsal unless he invites me. He can't invite me unless the author joins in the invitation. Even if I go, how can I interfere with the producer's work, or, being what I am, refrain from forgetting everything else and meddling all over the place? The company may dislike it, though, poor things, they dare not offend any author who may have a part to give them tomorrow. The producer might not mind if I could make suggestions to him to be handed on. But that is no use to me: I must *show* the actor what I want on the spur of the moment or as soon after as I can without interrupting.

As to the company not being aware of my presence you might as well try to conceal a giraffe in Piccadilly

171

Circus.

On the whole I dont think it a practical proposition, though I should like to see the play.

Where is the theatre? Beyond a vague notion that it is near Strand-on-the-Green I cannot locate it.

I am in London on Thursdays to Saturdays only; and on Thursdays I do not reach Kings Cross until 10.30.

I have heard nothing of Stella for a long time.

Nor of you, by the way. Your letter is the more welcome.

G.B.S.

The play compared well with many such drawing-room comedies, and several well-known actresses read it with a view to playing the lead, but economically the year 1933 was not a good one in which to find backers who would risk putting it on in the West End, and it did not reappear.

Before the end of the year, however, his second novel was published. He had intended to call it 'The Luck of the Drum', but again his publishers persuaded him to change the title, to *Fortune's Favourites*. It was the story of a greengrocer's family, suggested by that at the shop round the corner, who won the first prize in the (thinly disguised) Irish Sweepstake, the great gamble of the thirties, and of the havoc it wrought in their lives. It had scenes and characters in great variety: Cockney and Irish, Jew and Gentile, stage and stockbroking; true love and seduction, murder and retribution, town and country, and the country characters and settings were especially commended by reviewers. If his friends complained that it was sordid, they had to admit that he told a 'rattling good story'. Ideas flowed freely, he had little difficulty in inventing plots, but he was handicapped by a sentimentality inherent in the period in which he had grown up and in the work of many of the popular writers of his day.

172

XI ❧ Shaw Closes a Chapter

In the nineteen-thirties Cornwallis-West was convinced that a second war with Germany was inevitable. Discussing the prospect with an acquaintance, Gerald, known as 'Tim' Atkinson, who had many stage friends, he was reminded of the Lysistrata story, and immediately he began a play, with a contemporary setting, on the theme of women stopping war by a united effort of non-co-operation.

It was called 'The Woman Who Stopped War' and as usual he wrote to tell Shaw about it.

The theme was one after Shaw's own heart. Nearly twenty years earlier he had asked Stella 'why don't women rise up and say "We have the trouble of making these men; and if you don't stop killing them we shall refuse to make any more" '. A postcard reply came back:

4 Whitehall Court, London, S.W.1.
20th Oct. 1933.

Yes; but, damn it, she didn't stop it. However, send it along. I shall be at Ayot St Lawrence, Welwyn, Herts, until Thursday morning.

G.B.S.

The play was duly sent, and after a three months' wait Cornwallis-West received an overwhelming answer: a long letter of criticism and advice, a handwritten sheet of witty comment about meals on the stage, and his play, reduced by a whole act, with five characters eliminated, yet rearranged to form a five (instead of a four) act play, the alterations and directions all in Shaw's hand; and two closely-typed pages of dialogue giving the plot a completely different ending.

The theme of this ending, which was that of surrender, was predominant in Shaw's mind at the time and was elaborated by him in a broadcast a week or two later, on 6 February 1934, in the series 'Whither Britain?' In that talk he deduced from the failure of the League of Nations Disarmament Conference, which according to him had become an Armament Conference and had recently petered out, that disarmament would not prevent war: men fought before modern arms were invented; the only hope lay in making more, and more terrible, armaments and having 'very small armies highly trained to run away'. In face of the threat of bombing and poison gases all countries would surrender.*

4 Whitehall Court, London, S.W.1.
19th January 1934.

My dear George,

Here is your play cut to the right length and rearranged a bit.

If my operations startle you by their ruthlessness it may interest you to know that they are just about the same as the final cutting of On The Rocks. I always overwrite a play by at least a third. Ibsen wrote long stories about his characters and then dug a play out of them just as I write all sorts of things about my characters just to get to know them, and then dig a play out of them. This is your method, but you have not yet tumbled to the digging part of the business.

Also you have not broken yourself in to the limits imposed on the drama not only by its own nature, but

---

*Once the Second World War was a *fait accompli*, Shaw accepted the necessity to fight and prepared a broadcast on 'The Unavoidable Subject' in this sense. It was, however, banned by the then Minister of Information (Alfred Duff Cooper), according to Anthony Weymouth, who published it, with Shaw's permission, in his *Journal of the War Years*, Vol.1. Littlebury & Co., Worcester, 1948.

by time, space and money. You must get the play into 2½ hours, including intervals. You must not introduce characters who have to be paid from five to twenty pounds a week for two minutes work that a little ingenuity can dispense with. You must not try to make the stage do what it cannot do, though a newspaper or a novel can do it. You must not write a last act as though it were a first act: the two are quite different. A first act may be explanatory, introductory and full of little details to establish an atmosphere. All this must be dropped as the play goes on; the last half of it must move faster and faster, and concentrate on the few principals in whom the audience has become interested. The least attempt to check the pace or go back to the first act conditions is fatal. Also, unless you are writing a Comedy of Errors, you must not duplicate a leading character; to replace Othello and Iago by two Othellos would be to divide the interest.

The extent to which you have violated these canons is appalling; and I would exhort you to study my mutilations with them in mind.

Apart from these mechanical considerations, you have taken the liberty of making your heroine a woman of extraordinary and rather callous strength of mind and also a sentimental leading lady of East Lynne extraction crushed by a threatened separation from her chee-yild. This wont do. Mary acts as only a *maitresse-femme* could act; and she must go through with it. It is the man who must crumple up as a terrified sentimentalist.

The only way I could illustrate what I mean was by jotting down a lot of dialogue myself. It was much easier and shorter than trying to explain it: in fact it was the only way I could do it; but you can rehandle it your own way, taking care, however, not to make the

175

play any longer than I have left it.

I am starting for New Zealand on the 8th, and have had to hurry the job accordingly.

Always,

G. Bernard Shaw.

I find I have hardly succeeded in this. When you allow for the changes of scene and of dress (most important for Mary) it is dreadfully long for an 8.30 play. So cut as much as you can out of I,III & IV as you can [sic] without spoiling them. I have left them untouched.

The reference to 'an 8.30 play' and to getting the play 'into 2½ hours' reminds us that eight-thirty was the time at which almost all London performances began, until the air-raids of World War II forced on Londoners the earlier hours which have largely remained in force.

On the Rocks was a political comedy set in No. 10 Downing Street where the Cabinet is dealing, or failing to deal, with contemporary problems. Whatever his cutting of it, Shaw retained one sentence which was incidentally relevant to Cornwallis-West's play. When the prime minister remarks that he cannot go faster than the voters will let him, his wife exclaims:

Oh, your voters! What do they know about government? Football, prizefighting, war: that is what they like. And they like war because it isn't real to them: it's only a cinema show. War is real to me; and I hate it, as every woman to whom it is real hates it. But to you it is only part of your game.

The reference to the cutting of his own play is one more illustration of Shaw's courtesy, letting the novice know that his play had had the same treatment as his own. In a note in red ink on a half sheet of paper enclosed with the typescript of 'The Woman Who Stopped War', he wrote:

Meals on the stage are a fearful bother. The stalls, full to the neck, hate the smell of them and cannot sympathise with a display of appetite. The pit and gallery are seldom hungry enough to be tantalized. The actor *may* be hungry — I have known one who bargained for a stage meal; but that was at Margate — but a London actor should not be obliged to swallow a dictated meal which he may loathe. Banquets with property viands and goblets are quite in order; but unless (as in You Never Can Tell) a real meal has funny or interesting dramatic accompaniment, it is to be avoided.

I should take Tim and his meal off the stage, and get rid of page 9 with its disgusting steak and stout. Consider the vegetarians and teetotallers in front! It seems impossible to do this, as Tim must be on the stage to explain the plot. But there are two ways of doing it. 1. Avoid the meal altogether by making Tim explain that he has dined already conveying, if you like, that he really has no appetite. 2. Postpone the meal until the end of the act. This is easy.

In the preface to volume II of *Plays Pleasant and Unpleasant* Shaw explained the presence of the stage meal in *You Never Can Tell:*

You Never Can Tell was an attempt to comply with many requests for a play in which the much paragraphed "brilliancy" of *Arms and the Man* should be tempered by some consideration for the requirements of managers in search of fashionable comedies for West End theatres. I had no difficulty in complying, as I have always cast my plays in the ordinary practical comedy form in use in all the theatres; and far from taking an unsympathetic view of the popular preference for fun, fashionable dresses, a little music and even an exhibition of eating and drinking by people with an expensive-air, attended by an if-possible-comic waiter, I was more than willing to show that raw drama can humanize these things as easily as they, in undramatic hands, can dehumanize the drama.

The luncheon party in that play was the climax of Act II and the plot developed to the accompaniment of soup (thick or clear), turbot, an unnamed joint, salad, a 'cold sweet', cheese; with lager for the young men, apollonaris for the solicitor, who did not want anything heating, wine for the ladies, stone-ginger for the youngest daughter and, not disclosed to us until after the meal, seltzer and Irish whiskey for the erring father.

Cornwallis-West wrote immediately to thank Shaw and to ask for an opportunity of discussing his revolutionary suggestions in person before the Shaws left for New Zealand a few days later. In reply he received an appointment and another letter about his play:

4 Whitehall Court, London, S.W.1.

23rd Jany 1934

Dear G. C-W,

Could you make it 5.30 on Thursday at Whitehall Court? It is the only moment I can manage: this packing and settling up for three months absence is damnable.

Dont be afraid of Hard Hannah: I have proved that you can make her a heroine with complete impunity and immense celebrity. The dangerous heroine nowadays is the East Lynne lady torn from her child.

If you want to write a Walezska play (I think that was her name) by all means write it. If you want to write an H.H. play, you have written it. What you mustn't do is to begin with Hannah, and when you have led up to her K.O. blow, suddenly substitute Walezska (got it wrong that time, I think — or right) in miserable collapse. There were reasons why W. could not marry Napoleon. There are none why Mary should not marry Enthoven (what will Gabrielle say, by the way?) if she's a womanly woman and not a super H.H. And W.

178

didn't organize a world strike against war and carry public meetings off their feet.

Don't fall between two stools. No man, when he starts to write a play, knows how it will turn out on his hands. The result is often very disconcerting — at first.

Always yrs

G.B.S.

P.S. Why should Mary go back to an attic? She didn't come from one. It's an Elephant & Castle alternative.

Shaw's suggested ending, for surrender to the pressure not of women but of events, knocked the bottom out of Cornwallis-West's plot. Eventually he felt unable to accept it.

Perhaps their meeting convinced him that the difficulties of getting his play presented on the London stage would be too great, that the public were not ready for it. Perhaps he found the 'digging' process recommended in the previous letter too much for him; perhaps the hand of the master on his play had withered his own. Yet he was extremely anxious to use the idea to bring home to people the reality of the coming war, and so he left the play alone and resorted to the medium which he could handle best. The Shaws went off to New Zealand, and by the time they came back he had written a novel, retaining the title and his own plot of the play.

Knowing that Shaw was sympathetic to the theme and that his sponsorship could focus world attention on it if he chose, he asked if his friend would write a preface to the book.

This, unfortunately, was not an original thought. To quote Miss Patch: 'A short head behind the autograph hunters, writers in search of a preface were our next affliction . . .' and Shaw had to devise a stock postcard to deal with them to the effect that prefaces by him owed their value to the expectation of book purchasers that they would prove important works in themselves. 'A request for a preface by him was therefore ... a request for some months of hard professional work'.

4 Whitehall Court, London, S.W.1.
16th January 1935.

My dear C-W

Unfortunately this, which seems such a simple matter, is utterly, totally, completely and entirely out of the question. Read the enclosed stock postcard and you will see why.

But in any case it would be a senseless proceeding. Of course a publisher would like to get my circulation on top of yours. For that matter he would like to have half a dozen prefaces by well known authors. But if he were to say to you 'I will publish this if you can get a preface by Shaw, and not otherwise, you would be justified in punching his head for so gross a disparagement of your own publicity.

I am in a deuce of a mess just now; my wife ill in bed with an unaccountable temperature that wont come down, my projected voyage to South America called off, and the place full of doctors and nurses. However, my study, with Miss Patch in command, is still uninvaded if you blow in tomorrow.

Ever
G. Bernard Shaw

The card enclosed with this letter has disappeared.

The Woman Who Stopped War was published as a novel in this same year, 1935, by Hutchinson, who described it in the blurb as 'Vivid, provoking and brilliantly written'. The following year it went into a cheap edition. Its author had noticeably improved his style and had refrained from including too many subsidiary characters.

G.B.S., home from a second visit to South Africa, returned thanks for a copy, and revived the subject of Stella;

180

Malvern Hotel, Malvern
27th July 1935.

My dear C-W

Many thanks for the book and the inscription therein.

On my return from South Africa I found a letter from Hollywood which gave me a cue for replying urging very strongly the cruelty of the existing situation.

I wonder whether it will have any effect. Professional prospects out there are pretty desperate.

Always yours

G.B.S.

P.S. The Festival here, involving three of my plays, is working me to rags. I can only snatch a moment to write.

There had been a gap of nearly three years in the correspondence between Shaw and Stella, during which time she had gone to America to look for work and had marooned herself there rather than subject her Pekingese, Moonbeam, to the rigours of quarantine if she returned to England. Early in 1935 she had renewed contact with Shaw and the letter which he mentions as giving him 'a cue' was evidently that of 8 April 1935 in the published correspondence, giving a new Hollywood address. She enclosed her latest photograph so that he could see she really could play his Millionairess 'should you want me'. She was desperately in need of work and the film studios continually put her off. Meanwhile she had exhausted her allowance from Mrs Guinness before the next instalment was due and was constrained to ask his help, reminding him that by behaving 'like a gentleman' over his letters to her she had lost a fortune. The blandishments are familiar, the implications sad.

Shaw evidently took the opportunity of urging her to cease her futile hold-out on her husband and profit from the much needed income a divorce would bring her.

181

In each succeeding year from its inauguration until 1939, new plays of his, or revivals, were produced at the Malvern Festival. For the year 1935, in addition to revivals of *Fanny's First Play* and *Misalliance,* he contributed a new play, *The Simpleton of the Unexpected Isles,* written expressly for the Festival according to the description in the Festival brochure. It had, however, already had its first production at the Guild Theatre, New York, where it had a rough passage and the brochure opened with a long letter from Joseph Wood Krutch, editor of the New York *Nation,* making a kind of tolerant apologia for the play, followed by Shaw's even longer, and delightful, reply. Earlier, he had chided Stella for one of her tactical blunders in snubbing the illustrious Guild Theatre thereby losing her chance of a part in this play.

His letter pleading 'the cruelty of the existing situation' had no effect, and both he and Cornwallis-West must have realised that, if the possibility of more money would not move her though she so much needed it, certainly no other consideration would. She could not forgive her husband for the fact that the refusal to continue their life together had come from him and not from herself.

In the hope that the success of the novel might after all open the way for the appearance of his play on the stage, where he felt its message would reach a wider public, Cornwallis-West approached several people whom he knew in the theatrical world and who agreed to read it.

Owen Nares, famous actor-manager of the twenties and thirties, summed up the main difficulties from the practical point of view:

> I was very interested by your play, which I consider to be most admirably written and carried out.
>
> Of course propaganda is a very dangerous and difficult subject to handle for the stage and I am afraid this

is the reason your play has not yet been produced. As regards myself, the fact that it is a woman's play, added to the quality of propaganda, makes it impossible to suggest a production.

Leonora Corbett, though anxious to play the lead, also found it impossible to arrange the production. A family friend and talented actress, Mary Newcomb, who had received 'a passionate letter from Rosita McGrath' (intrepid traveller of the thirties) about it, thought the idea a splendid one which 'came off' in the book but, in the play, was swamped by the plot.

Finally, looking around for the necessarily rich and idealistic backer who might risk a production in the cause of world peace, he sent a copy of the book to the eccentric millionairess, Lady Houston, whose philanthropy in causes that appealed to her was frequently reported in the press and who had bought the *Saturday Review* in order that it should express her views. They proved to be more conventional than the methods proposed in the book. From her yacht at Sandbanks, Dorset, she wrote:

I received your very interesting book — 'The Woman Who Stopped War' — and have read it with great interest. I only wish that your good idea could materialise — it is badly needed just now — but the way to stop War is to be twice as strong as any other Nation as it was in the good old days.

Sadly he laid the play aside, convinced that the time would come all too soon when its topicality would be demonstrated.

In January 1936 Edward VIII succeeded to the throne and within a few months there was a riot of gossip and rumour about the sovereign's determination to maintain a private life rather different from the exigencies of his public one. With a view to alleviating the vulgarity of it all, Cornwallis-West wrote an article no copy of which, unfortunately, survives, destined for *The Saturday Evening Post.* He sent it to the King for his approval, and received a piquant if unorthodox reply. On a used foolscap envelope, postmarked, over George V stamps, '21 Apr 36', address-ed to Mrs Simpson at Bryanston Court, W.1.,H.M. had jotted down in red pencil a brief but appreciative message signed with his initials. Though mollified by the kind re-mark, the recipient was perplexed by this break with the traditions of royal correspondence to which he had been accustomed.

The routine of the seasons continued: an occasional day's racing, a visit to Lords, or a game of golf provided a chance to be out of doors. So did weekends with old friends, at lovely Ramsbury Manor, the home of Sir Francis Burdett; at Barton Court, the Berkshire home of Colonel 'Minor' Lawson, the 3rd Lord Burnham, and at historic Broadlands, Lord Palmerston's old home in Hampshire, where Lord and Lady Mount Temple lived.

In the spring the Irish rivers summoned him, and at the end of the summer season, a day or so before the Twelfth, in a car packed with books, rods, guns and tweeds of ancient vintage, he would set off, with Campbell happily trans-formed from butler to loader, for the north, buoyant at the prospect of feeling his feet in the heather and hearing again the gossip of the ghillies and stalkers whom he knew almost as well as he knew their employers, his hosts. Glene-tive, Invercauld, Suisgill, Kildonan, Glen Quoich, he loved them all, and especially Strathconon, then belonging to the Combes, and Lochmore, his brother-in-law Bend Or's estate, as being the best stalking forests in Scotland. Apart from fishing, deer-stalking was the sport which gave him greatest satisfaction, not only for the finesse it demanded but also for the hours spent alone among the hills.

A violently impatient man in some circumstances, he could happily spend the best part of a day pitting his brains against a stag's power of sight and smell, or kneel motionless on a bank or stand for an hour in a stream awaiting the pleasure of an elusive trout, taking in, meanwhile, the busy-ness of voles, moor hen, water rats, kingfishers and flies.

By the time he headed south again pheasant shooting would be coming in, and from then until Christmas his skill with a gun ensured him regular invitations for shooting parties with old friends, beginning with Lord Fitzwilliam's at vast, sooty Wentworth Woodhouse. In fact the Edwardian tradition of *perpetuo mobile* still prevailed, and after Christmas, when winter ills usually began to attack him if he delayed, he would set off with his sister Shelagh or with friends, in search of sunshine, to the South of France or on a cruise to the East or to South America.

On one of these voyages he met Miss Kathleen Barker, the well-known animal artist, and enlisted her interest in the production of a book which he had had in mind for years, an affectionate tribute to dogs he had owned or known. He wrote the story, she illustrated it delightfully, and the result was an appealing book, *Us Dogs,* being the autobiography of Sambo, a Labrador, which was published in England by *Country Life* and in New York by Scribners, in 1938. It appeared in time for the Christmas market, bringing him a flood of letters from fellow dog lovers.

A few years earlier, after enjoying *Edwardians Go Fishing,* the late 6th Duke of Portland had sent him a copy of his own *Fifty Years of Sport in Scotland,* with a letter apologising for its 'horrible size and beastly bulk', it being a heavy, sumptuously produced and illustrated, truly magnificent volume. Cornwallis-West now sent him a copy of *Us Dogs* and in reply received a four-page letter from the Duke, from Berriedale, Caithness, in his very large, distinctive hand:

Thank you very much indeed for sending me the quite

185

delightful book which you have so very cleverly written. I read it until 2 o'clock this a.m. and now my wife has collared it and I am sure will never give it up. I can't tell you how much we like it — so much that I hope you will order a *dozen* copies more to be sent to us to give to the people here. This won't spoil your sale as most probably they will not have the chance of buying it.

The author was amused by what he interpreted as a request for a dozen free copies for the ducal Christmas presents.

Stella had spent much of the nineteen-thirties in France or America, and chiefly in America. In her later years she exercised her notorious fascination on various young men of the day, through whose books she sails, or erupts, according to the circumstances and her mood.

Edward Marsh had known her nearly all his life and quoted some of her flashes of wit in his autobiography. Osbert Sitwell had a tolerant recollection of her on a rough Atlantic crossing in 1926, in his book *Laughter in the Next Room:*

By itself the force of the elements would have made one ponder on the relative immensities of space and man: but hardly less so did the occasional fair-weather materialisations, in the chair next me, of my witty, bubble-pricking friend, Mrs Patrick Campbell, who appeared with a little the air of a luminous-faced seal. What she most enjoyed in conversation was to see how far she could go, like a child playing Tom Tiddler's Ground; without being caught — without being hurt. Sometimes, however, she hurt others in the process.

In Noel Coward's *Present Indicative* there are several glimpses of her, including a typical one of her cadging, in her inimitable way, an invitation to the dress rehearsal of *The Constant Nymph,* on the ground that she couldn't

186

afford a ticket when it opened, and ringing him up the next morning to tell him, commiseratingly, that he was the wrong type for the play.

John Gielgud, a devoted admirer of her talent, recalled in *Early Stages* that in 1931 she agreed provisionally to play in his production of Rodney Ackland's *Strange Orchestra:*

> When the first rehearsal . . . began, Mrs Pat pretended she did not understand the play. 'Who are all these extraordinary characters?' she demanded. 'Where do they live? Does Gladys Cooper know them?' She invariably arrived late every morning and we would hear her talking loudly all the way from the stage-door . . . In the end she left us and I was in despair. She had rehearsed the part magnificently.

The American journalist, Alexander Woollcott, devoted an entertaining chapter to her in *While Rome Burns.*

It was Cecil Beaton who gave a final description of her in New York in the last year of her life, beautifully gauging her imbalance between the sublime and the ridiculous. She came to him to be photographed, in her black velvet and artificial pearls, with her white Pekingese on her lap, 'a prototype of a stage duchess. But after the hot lights had played on her for a while, she began to disintegrate. There was something ghastly about her dirty white gloves, her fallen chins and the tragic impediments of age'. He took her to lunch at Voisin's. 'She was in good form castigating Orson Welles' production of *Julius Caesar.*' Beaton did not think a great deal of the pictures he had taken of her, but to her, when she saw them, 'they seemed the distillation of magic. "Oh, that shadow under the jaw! You're a genius to put in that shadow. And no one has taken such a photograph of gloved hands. Those gloves are alive." '

She talked to him at some length about the actors and actresses she had known, and about the pupils whom she was at the moment training in voice production and speak-

187

ing. At their next meeting Beaton was himself taking a lesson from her in this art. The day was her seventy-third birthday. As he was shown up to her room, 'a wiry old fox' (evidently the late Gabriel Wells, to whom she was comtemplating selling Shaw's letters at an extortionate price) was being shown out. She indicated the letters, filed in packets in her desk. 'Oh, if only he would buy them and see that they were properly treated . . . but it's all so difficult.'

Later that year she returned to Europe, living for a few months in Paris. The correspondence with Shaw had continued at intervals, he still trying to give her good advice about their letters, she reminding him of their battles in the theatre long ago. His last letter to her was dated 31 August 1939. In the spring of 1940 she was ill with pneumonia, and on 9 April 1940 she died, at Pau in the Pyrenees.

The report of the memorial service for her in London appeared in *The Times* on the same day as the announce-ment of her husband's third marriage to Mrs Georgette Hirsch, a friend of some years' standing, widow of Adolph Hirsch of South Africa. He had waited twenty years for his release from Stella; her refusal to give it was not from love but from wounded vanity. Now he celebrated his freedom. The appearance of the announcements on the same day was accidental, but it made the position clear to anyone who still did not know it.

Shaw's last letter to him on the subject of Stella, dated 26 February 1941, reached him at Branksome where driven out of London by air raids, he and his wife, were staying. It runs to six hundred words. Unfortunately the Society of Authors, who, under the Public Trustee, act for the Shaw Estate, have refused their permission for me to quote this, the most important of the letters given to me by the recipient, as their literary adviser in America,

188

Professor Dan H. Lawrence, to whom photo copies were referred and who is editing Shaw's letters, I understand intends to publish it first in his own work.

It was written at the time of the fiercest German bombing of London when, as Shaw implied, people were always glad to hear that their friends were still alive. Even the village of Ayot St Lawrence had been bombed and at night they could watch London burning thirty miles away.

Then he settled down to speak for the last time about the woman who had made so great an impact on both their lives. The sale of her furniture was coming up at Harrods, and though it might seem a good idea for him to buy it for her daughter, who had lost by bombing everything she possessed, he believed it would be a far greater kindness to let her have the proceeds of the sale to help her start a new life of her own, free from the shackles of the past and of having been overshadowed by so famous a mother. In fact the process of getting rid of the past was completed by the total destruction of Harrods' sale records by bombing later in the year.

Stella's will had figured prominently in the press and, concerned as always for his wife's feelings, he had carefully selected the press cuttings she saw. Shaw was a realist in everything. As is known from his attitude to the deaths of his mother and sister, he scorned to adopt a tone different from that which he would have used in speaking of them during their lives. He had no use for the unctuous half-truths current at such times. He spoke of her poverty at the end, of her losing the will to live, of her obstinacy and her constant pressure on him to let her sell his letters to her and so at last outshine the Ellen Terry correspondence which had been published in 1931. Yet now that she was dead his conscience smote him lest he seemed to be depriving her daughter of the money she could make by their publication.

He believed she bore no malice for his professedly rough treatment of her in their last exchange of letters; but at the time she made her will the last sentence of it must surely have been designed in a mood of exquisite malice to cancel out all that Shaw had been careful to say in *The Apple Cart* about their relationship. For according to *The Times* report the will ended:

> . . . it is my desire that the copyright be free or permission be obtained, that the Bernard Shaw letters and poems . . . be published in an independent volume to be entitled 'The Love Letters of Bernard Shaw to Mrs Patrick Campbell' so that all who read them will realise that the friendship was *l'amitie amoureuse.*

From Shaw's last letter to her it appeared that Gabriel Pascal had offered her a part in the film of *Pygmalion* which he directed with Wendy Hiller in the role of Eliza, but that she lost it because again she would not be parted from her dog. Nearly thirty years earlier, setting out on her triumphal progress with *Pygmalion* to New York and needing a little dog, her 'trade mark', to take with her, it was her daughter-in-law Helen's that she 'borrowed' in its owner's absence, so ensuring that it would be he and not her own dog that would be consigned to quarantine on her return.

At the end of his long letter to George, after a comment on his increasing age, Shaw reverted to the permanently insoluble problem which still harassed them both: war, and enclosed a pamphlet on the government's suppression of *The Daily Worker.*

Thus Shaw closed the chapter that had made so great an impact on the lives of George Cornwallis-West and of himself.

XII ❧ Vanished Turquoise

George Cornwallis-West had a strong sense of the super-natural and was convinced that he had had genuine psychic experiences. He claimed to have seen the ghost of Nell Gwynne at Salisbury Hall and to have been driven from his bed by spectral manifestations in the haunted room at Furstenstein. Under anaesthesia during an operation in America he had a curious 'dream' which he later wrote down in detail and showed to Sir Shane Leslie, who thought the account merited being sent to the Society of Psychical Research. 'Ghosts are part of our lives' commented Sir Shane, 'and I should be sorry to be without them'.

A note from Winston Churchill in July 1940 thanked him, understandably briefly in view of what he had on his hands at that time, for his letter recalling a past discussion on prayer. 'I will bear what you say in mind,' he wrote, and no doubt that omnivorous mind did retain it, pigeon-holed along with the affairs of the nation. I remember visiting George with some books one wintry afternoon when he was laid up with one of his many ills. As I was leaving he said, half whimsically but a trifle anxiously, 'Do you think God will forgive me if I say my prayers in bed tonight?'

At some time in his later life he made a change in his tiepin. For years he had worn his father's large and decorative turquoise and gold pin such as would have warmed the heart of Sir Harold Nicolson. It was absolutely right for him, a period emblem in an increasingly anonymous society, but one day it vanished. He had been gently

191

teased for being old-fashioned and he could not stand much teasing, so one day he took his beloved old pin to the jewellers' and returned, devoid of its characteristic *panache,* with a circlet of minute diamonds in a plain platinum setting, neat and not gaudy but ludicrously insignificant for its height and breadth. It seemed somehow symbolic of the narrowing horizon.

He had looked forward to continuing to write, but the Second World War, breaking out in 1939, put an end to that and for the next few years he and his wife lived in a Bournemouth hotel. He suffered acutely, in common with other active men of his age, from the feeling of uselessness, and the shortage of petrol reduced him to pottering, until Field Marshal Alexander* helped him to obtain some in order to deliver lectures at Home Guard centres and, when that petered out, to get to the nearest river. Fishing the Avon at Christchurch remained his only consolation and he gave the results, usually pike, to the matron of a local institution, happily oblivious, as I noticed when on a visit, of the look of consternation which belied her murmured thanks when a hugh muddy fish was laid in her arms with the warning that it should be disembowelled immediately. There were some red letter days when salmon were the catch.

He thought nostalgically of his familiar treasures put away in store. 'I often wonder whether I shall ever cast eyes again on my well-loved Lares and Penates' he wrote to me. 'At times I don't think I shall, and that is why I have explained where the things are that I would love you to have. I have added two letters from my friend F.M. Alexander . . . No more royalties from my novels but the demand for the dog book is everlasting and cannot be fulfilled until after the war'.

I had recommended for his booklist Lady Carbery's

*later Earl Alexander of Tunis.

reminiscences and, when he had read them, received a characteristic reply:

Happy World is quite the most charming book I have read for a very long time . . . It brings my own childhood back to me, except that as you know mine was by no means a happy one. I too had vague wonderings, and when I could not get any satisfactory explanation used to invent my own. I had a favourite tree which I used to call my Engine Tree . . . I had pet names for many flowers . . . a wild violet was a Peep-eye because it always seemed to be looking out of its leaves shyly; not boldly. A cowslip I called a Smell-sweet, and a bluebell a Cry-baby, because it drooped its head and was covered with dew. So you can imagine how the book appealed to me. It took me back six decades.

Occasionally he spent a few hours in London. One day I remember, when we lunched together, he was on his way to see his former cook-housekeeper who, to his great distress, was seriously ill in hospital. In the dreariness of the wartime streets his was still a figure to make people turn their heads and look a second time at his six foot three inches, his perfect carriage, patrician poise of the head, fresh complexion and direct blue-eyed gaze. Handsome, resilient, engaging, with an enormous capacity for enjoying the simple pleasures of life, picnics, mutton pies, the dart of a kingfisher across a stream, the solemnity of young children, the posturing of the pompous, he saw the joke in nearly everything, though, like most shy people he was inordinately sensitive. I was reminded of this by a passage in *Grace and Favour* in which the author is speaking of the lasting effects of an unhappy childhood:

Those who are not afflicted by shyness think of it as a mere nothing, even a pose. They do not realise that it is a sort of permanent ache, poisoning all human relationships and that, however much one may ignore it, there it always is, ready to spring up and cast its blight.

There it always was. I sometimes thought that it was shyness which prompted nature genuinely to raise the temperature and produce symptoms of sickness necessitating a retreat to bed when a stranger had, in a rash moment, been invited to luncheon or dinner.

'Most of us are shaped by our childhood', wrote André Maurois concerning Stendhal. 'By the time he is eight a man has become either an optimist or a pessimist. He changes very little after that unless events bring him a maturity of great happiness after a childhood of great misery, or vice versa, and even so there will always remain something of melancholy and timidity in the make-up of those whose beginnings were inauspicious.'

The war closed in. Bereavements came thick and fast. Sons of old friends were killed in action, including Sir Thomas Watson, the eldest son of the family he had watched over in their childhood. In 1943 he lost his very dear friend Lord Burnham, to whom he had dedicated *Edwardians Go Fishing* in token of happy hours spent together on the Kennet. In the same year his elder sister died in Germany after a long illness from which, he had known for years, only death could release her. From Lochmore he wrote:

> I am back at one of my old haunts, staying with Westminster. *The Times* gave my sister Daisy a wonderful obituary notice and the account of the memorial service was . . . representative of 'Edwardian Hey-Days,' days when I used to come up here a lot. I rode 8 miles the other day to fish a loch, over hills and through corries where I used to stalk deer in the early nineteen-hundreds . . . Apart from the sport, it is such a blessing and so peaceful to get away from what an old farm labourer described to me as 'Them there bloody war noises'.

194

There was a distressing sequel to Princess Daisy's death when in 1946 news came of the wholesale looting of the castle of Furstenstein and the desecration of family tombs by Russian and Polish forces. Her superb collection of jewels had already been confiscated by the Poles in a previous raid.

By then the war had ended but the life he had known was annihilated. He and his wife returned to a furnished flat in London while they looked for a permanent home, her house in Hill Street having been bombed and his given up. For a time he kept on his room in Bournemouth as he still had a gun in a syndicate near Ringwood. 'I just couldn't stick being in London week in and week out', he wrote, 'I should become old and doddery, just a Club loafer, the one thing I have always dreaded'; but inevitably when the subscription to the syndicate ran out it was not renewed, and only the walk to the Turf Club, though not to 'loaf' for long, remained. His wife relieved the boredom of post-war London with her keen interest in bridge, but although he enjoyed a game he never could spend long house at the card table. He confessed to suffering from intense depression. 'I suppose that during the war one kept up one's spirits by thinking "Well, it can't last much longer and we are bound to win, then things will improve". Now the war is over things are a darn sight worse . . . I really hate this world now, chiefly because of its appalling vulgarity'.

The aftermath of the war years was showing its effect on him in recurrent bouts of illness of one kind or another. Occasionally he suffered such severe pain as to require injections of morphia. He was also plagued by ingrowing eyelashes and, increasingly, by deafness and insomnia.

In November 1950 Shaw slipped quietly away, and with him the last link with the exciting artistic and creative life whose fringes he had touched and the stimulus of a great man's friendship.

After a serious illness he set off alone on a round trip of Africa by sea, but was taken ill on the first day out and was laid up for sixteen days in a small cabin. When he was about again, in his weak condition he found that neither the passengers nor the food were to his liking. 'I just couldn't stick it,' he wrote to me, 'so flew back from Dar-es-Salaam. The ship's doctor and the few friends I had made told me I was mad and that my heart wouldn't stand it, etc., etc. I had a lovely trip, 6,800 miles in 28 hours!! in a new Hermes plane, air-conditioned throughout, and I felt all the better for it'.

Excitement, novelty, adventure; a bit of a dare, in fact the sort of thing he might have done fifty years earlier if planes had been in use, was a tonic, the elixir of life, but more than twenty-eight hours were needed to keep it up. 'Not too well now in the cold weather,' this February letter continued. 'My legs are rotten and I stumble along on two sticks.' The doctors diagnosed Parkinson's Disease.

The bright day was done. Lying in the darkened room he had too much time to remember the mountain top from the nursery window, the Wild West Show, the captains and the kings and the fair women, all the beauty and gaiety and activity which however meretricious it might seem to those outside the charmed circle had been vital and precious to those within it. Spring was approaching, and he knew that never again would he be able to take his rod to the river. He never could bear waiting. On the first Sunday in April 1951, while his wife and the nurse were at lunch, he rose from his bed and with superhuman strength got down his revolver from a cupboard, loaded it and took the only way out.

196

❧ Index

197

151; Lady Cynthia Asquith on, 140; Cecil Beaton on, 186; Mrs Cornwallis-West on, 126; Noel Coward on, 185-186; John Gielgud on, 186; Lady Violet Greville on, 109; Mrs Lyttelton on, 116, 151; Edward Marsh on, 186; Hesketh Pearson on, 142; Athene Seyler on, 151; Shaw on, 118, 119, 161, 162, 163, 189, 190; Osbert Sitwell on, 186; Helen Spinola on, 110; Angela Thirkell on, 107; Alexander Woollcott on, 187

Campbell, the butler, 157, 158, 159, 184

Campbell, Helen (Marchesa Spinola), 110, 141, 190

Campbell, Patrick, 108-109, 110

Carbery, Lady, 192, 193

Carlton Hotel, 98, 99, 100

Carpentier, Georges, 138

Caruso, Enrico, 97, 166, 167

Cassel, Sir Ernest, 81, 82, 101

Castellane, Marquis 'Boni' de, 71

Cézanne, Paul, 99

Chamberlain, Joseph, 57

Chamberlain, Mrs Joseph, 74

Chambers, Haddon, 154, 155

Chapman-Huston, Desmond, 131

Churchill, Clementine Spencer-, Baroness, see Hozier, Clementine

Churchill, Ivor, 93

Churchill, Jennie, see Churchill, Lady Randolph

Churchill, John S., 64, 78, 92, 95, 103, 104

Churchill, Randolph S., 11, 12, 13, 69, 80

Churchill, Lord Randolph, 11, 56, 66; meets Jennie Jerome,

52; their romance, 52; enters Parliament, 53; marries, 54; offends Prince of Wales, 55; the Churchills are exiled to Ireland, 55; deep influence of the Irish experience, 57; the Churchills return to England, 57; Lady Dorothy Nevill on, 58; reconciliation with Prince of Wales, 58; helps to found the Primrose League, 58; appointed Secretary of State for India, 58; becomes Chancellor of the Exchequer and Leader of the House of Commons, 60; Lady Paget on, 60, 61; his sudden resignation from the cabinet, 60; visits Russia, 61; Jennie on, 62; goes to S.Africa in search of 'sport, gold and health', 62: estrangement from Jennie, 62; begins world tour, 62; collapses in India and returns home, 62; death, 64

Churchill, Lady Randolph, (Jennie), 11, 39, 46, 83, 84, 87, 88, 92, 157; family and childhood, 50-52; Jerome family comes to England, 52; she meets the Prince of Wales, 52; and Lord Randolph Churchill, 52; their romance, 52; marries, 54; love of gambling, 54; birth of son Winston, 55; her husband offends Prince of Wales, 55; the Churchills are exiled to Ireland, 55; their return to England, 57; flair for furnishing and decorating houses, 57; on the 'Professional Beauties', 26-27; on Mrs Cornwallis-West, 23; on Lillie

199

201

Cornwallis, Col. William, (George's father), 11, 31, 32, 86, 104, 129, 130, 141, 156, 191; ancestry, 11, 15-19, 34, 35, 36, 41; birth, childhood and youth, 19; his Italian daughters, 15; marriage, 20; interests, temperament and friends, 28, 132, 144; birth of George and his English daughters, 15, 20; George's affection for, 13; an enlightened father, 109; financial difficulties, 21; brings a libel action to defend his wife, 27; as member of parliament, 29; love of Ruthin Castle, 29; attitude to his wife 20, 30, 132-133, 143-144; keeps George short of money, 30, 31, 80; inherits the Cornwallis estates, 34, 145; architectural plans for Milford, 39, 145-146; donates a recreation ground to Ruthin, 47; seriously worried by George's infatuation with Jennie, 71; opposition to George marrying Jennie, 72; letter to Leonie Leslie concerning his son, 75-76; is suspected of pro-German sympathies, 125; reaction to public scandal involving his wife, 132-133; cartoon of, by 'Spy', 157; death and burial, 133

Cornwallis, Mrs William (George's mother; née FitzPatrick; known as Patsy): 11, 21, 22, 23, 24, 25, 26, 32, 44, 46, 68, 86, 152, 156, 157; her childhood 143; her marriage, 20; birth of her children, 15, 20; relations with George, 13, 26, 30, 144; her children left to the care of servants, 30; Lady Randolph Churchill on, 23; Lillie Langtry on, 24; celebrated by Count Beust, 25; and by Abraham Hayward, 25, 26; Lady Troubridge on, 26; a 'Professional Beauty', 27; subject of a vulgar canard, 27; stinginess of herself and her husband, 30, 31, 80; feud with her mother-in-law, 36, 37; her talent for design, 39; inconcerned by savagery at her son's school, 39; she and her husband seriously worried by George's infatuation with Jennie; 71; a keen yachts-woman, 71; opposition to George marrying Jennie, 71 fails to attend her son's wedding, 78; a demanding wife, 80; the Marchioness of Curzon on, 86; Patsy on Stella and Jennie, 126; letter to Stella, 127-128; her eccentricity in money matters, 128; becomes unpopular for helping German prisoners, 129; and the subject of a public scandal of a different kind, 130-133; death, 143; Princess Daisy on, 144; her son on, 144

Cowans, Sir John, 124, 130, 131
Coward, Sir Noel, 186, 187
Cox & Co., 115
Craigie, Mrs Pearl ('John Oliver Hobbes'), 65, 70, 149
Curzon, Lady Georgiana, 59
Curzon, of Kedleston, Marquess, 93
Curzon, Marchioness, 67, 85, 87
Cust, Lionel, 69

D'Abernon, Lord, 44-45, 61
D'Annunzio, Gabriele, 94
Daudet, Alphone, 99

Gladstone, William Ewart, 26, 53, 57, 96, 144, 148
Glyndwr, Owen, 16
Goncourt brothers, 99
Goodman, Dr Gabriel, 30
Goschen, Lord, 57
Granby, Marchioness of, see Rutland, Duchess of,
Granier, Jeanne, 94
Greet, Ben, 109
Grenville, Sidney, 94
Greville, Mrs Ronnie, 82
Greville, Lady Violet, 109
Grey, Sir Edward, 123
Grossmith, George jnr, 156
Grosvenor, Countess, 86
Grosvenor, Lady Ursula, 86
Guest, F.G., 114
Guinness, Mrs Benjamin, 150, 181
Gwynne, Nell, 92, 191

Hahn, Reynaldo, 97-98
Hall, Clara, see Jerome, Mrs Clara
Hamilton, Col. Ian, 49
Hans Heinrich XI, see Pless, Duke of
Hans Heinrich XV, see Pless, Prince of
Hardy, Thomas, 90
Harris, Frank, 164
Hawksmoor, Nicholas, 92
Hawthorne, Nathaniel, 19
Hayward, Abraham, 25, 26
Hazlitt, William, 19
Headfort, Thomas 2nd Marquess of, 20
Headfort, Marchioness of (Formerly Rose Boote), 87
Henry III, 41
Henry, VII, 16
Herbodeau, Eugène, 99
Herring, George, 82

Hichens, Robert, 115
Hiller, Wendy, 190
Hirsch, Adolph, 188
Hirsch, Baron, 81
Hirsch, Mrs Georgette, see Cornwallis-West, Mrs Georgette
Ho Chi Minh, 98
Home, Daniel Dunglas, 19
Hood, Vice-Admiral Sir Samuel, 35
Hoppner, J., 34, 157
Houston, Lady, 183
Howes, Mr and Mrs, 89
Hozier, Lady Blanche, 95
Hozier, Clementine (later Churchill), 95, 104
Hunt, Leigh, 19
Huntington, Mr, 165

Ibsen, Henrik, 174
Iddesleigh, Countess of, 58
Ingram, Rex, 157, 165
Irving, Henry, 23
Ismay, Bower, 128

Jackson, Sir Barry, 162
James, Henry, 70
James, Mr and Mrs Willie, 89, 94
Janotha, Mlle, 65
Jerome, Camille, 51
Jerome, Mrs Clara (née Hall), 50, 51, 52, 55, 65
Jerome, Clara, see Frewen, Clara
Jerome, Jennie, see Churchill, Lady Randolph
Jerome, Leonard, 50, 51, 52, 53, 55, 65
Jerome, Leonie, see Leslie, Leonie
John, King of France, 16
Johnson, Jack, 138
Johnson, Dr Samuel, 16, 70

209

George, 121-123, 160, 161, 162, 163, 164, 167, 168, 169, 171, 172, 173, 174-176, 177, 178-179, 180, 181, 188-190; criticism of George's writings, 12, 135-139, 154-155, 172, 173, 174-177, 178-179; on war, 123, 174 & n.; his Open Letter to President of the U.S., 123; attends a reading of George's first play, 135; learns Stella's version of her marriage, 149; but sympathises with George, 149; acts as mediator between Stella and George, 12, 149, 150, 181; recipient of her diatribes and his plaints, 150; attitude to suggested film of his life, 164; advice on retaining film rights, 165; reply to George's invitation to attend rehearsal of his play, 171-172; on Stella's autobiography, 159, 160; on her, 118, 119, 161, 162, 163, 189, 190; on authors in search of a preface, 180; association with Malvern Festival, 161, 181, 182; Stella renews contact with, and he urges her to grant George a divorce, 181, 182; last letter to Stella, 188; letters to Ellen Terry, 189; death, 195

Sheridan, Clare (née Frewen), 65, 66, 94, 148

Sheridan, Wilfred, 94

Simpson, Mrs (later Duchess of Windsor), 184

Sitwell, Sir Osbert, 71, 186

Smith, F.E., see Birkenhead, Lord

Society of Authors, 188

Society of Psychical Research, 191

Somerset, Lady Henry, 57

Spinola, Marchesa, see Campbell, Helen

'Spy', 157

Squire, Ronald, 170

Stendhal, 194

Stern, G.B., 163

Stowe, Harriet Beecher, 19

Strong, Arthur, 69

Succi, the fasting man, 40, 41

Sutherland, Millicent Duchess of, 47

Sutro, Alfred, 89

Swinburne, Algernon, 70

Sykes, Christopher, 113

Tempest, Marie, 170

Tennyson, Frederick, 19

Terry, Ellen, 23, 189

Tetrazzini, 113

Thirkell, Angela, 107

Thrale, Mrs, 16

Torby, Countess, 67

Tree, Sir Herbert Beerbohm, 119

Troubridge, Laura Lady, 26, 57-58

Turner, Reggie, 97

Tweedmouth, Lady, 89

Verdi, Giuseppe, 70

Victoria, Queen, 39, 45, 47, 55, 59, 60, 70, 85, 103, 112

von Hohenthal, Countess Walburga, see Paget, Lady

Wales, Edward Prince of, 11, 22, 23, 38, 39, 40, 42, 49, 52, 54, 55, 58, 65, 70, 71, 72, 75, 77, 95, 98, 113; see also Edward VII

Wales, Princess of, 42, 54, 55, 58; see also Alexandra, Queen

Walewska, Marie, Countess Colonna, 178

211